RAW JUICE

Shows how fresh fruit and vegetable juices promote increased
health and vitality.

RAW JUICES
FOR HEALTH

Prepared and produced by the Editorial Committee of
Science of Life Books

Revised and expanded by
Vivienne Lewis

SCIENCE OF LIFE BOOKS
11 Munro Street, Port Melbourne, Victoria 3207

Second Edition, revised,
enlarged and reset 1985

© SCIENCE OF LIFE BOOKS 1985

*Registered at the G.P.O. Sydney
for transmission through the post
as a book*

*This book is sold subject to the condition that it shall not, by way of
trade or otherwise, be lent, re-sold, hired out, or otherwise circulated
without the publisher's prior consent in any form of binding or cover
other than that in which it is published and without a similar
condition including this condition being imposed on the subsequent
purchaser.*

Inquiries should be made to the publishers:
Lothian Publishing Company Pty. Ltd.
11 Munro Street, Port Melbourne, 3207

U.K. Distributors:
THORSONS PUBLISHING GROUP
Wellingborough, Northamptonshire

U.S.A. Distributors:
THORSONS PUBLISHERS INC.
New York

National Library of Australia card number
and ISBN 0-909911-11-8

Printed and bound in Great Britain

Contents

Introduction

Many writers on nutrition have become almost poetical on the subject of raw, fresh juice. They attribute more than just pure goodness and an abundance of vitamins, minerals and other nutrients to the juices extracted from fruits and vegetables. They believe that raw juices radiate a life-force all of their own. Certainly there is no better recipe for instant vitality and a feeling of well-being than to take regularly a glass of fruit or vegetable juice, freshly pressed.

Juices contain vitamins and minerals, plus enzymes, that are absorbed into the bloodstream and get to work on the body within minutes. This makes them a wonderful tonic for tiredness, for cleaning out the system and starting the day fresh, alert and full of energy. Whether they are taken as a pick-you-up or as part of an intensive therapy to treat a specific illness, fresh raw juices are 'powerhouses' of nutrients, getting to work on the body quickly and safely.

It is not just a fad that health farms and spas use the raw juice cure (called the *Rohsaft Kur*), as to take nothing but juice is probably the most efficient way of reducing fatigue and stress. Drinking nothing except juices extracted from fresh fruit and vegetables enables the body to fight against the accumulation of waste-matter and toxins which gradually poison the system. By going on a raw juice fast, the digestive system is given a chance to rest, the whole body can start to resist and kill off dead or diseased cells, and resistance to future infections can begin. Indeed, raw juices have been successfully used to treat all kinds of illnesses.

It is probably not realized how many energy-giving calories are packed into natural fresh juices. The calorie content of a litre of grape or pineapple juice is between 800 and 900 calories. To get the same amount of calories from other foods it would be necessary to eat approximately a dozen eggs or 3 pints (1½ litres) of milk, 3 lb (1.4 kilos) potatoes, or 1½ lb (650g) of meat. Apple juice contains 500 calories per litre, while cherry juice and pear juice have a little less, and orange juice contains 400 calories per litre.

Locked into fruits and vegetables are millions of cells containing vitamins, minerals, enzymes and other nutrients, those known and those yet to be identified. Raw juices have none of the dangerous side-effects of modern drugs but they can be used as a medicine to repair the damage done to our bodies by rushed meals and unhealthy eating habits, brought about by the pressures of modern life.

With our over-processed foods, we take in too much acid which poisons our bodies and causes poor health. We should be aiming at an intake of mostly alkaline foods, which includes raw fruits and vegetables, and these should be ripened before picking. The acid-forming foods are the over-refined white flour and white sugar foods, laced with too much salt and fat, white bread, commercially-produced biscuits and cakes, as seen on all the supermarket shelves and, of course, sweets. These foods do not exercise our teeth to start with and without chewing very much we do not get the digestive juices working properly. This sort of food clogs the system and the bloodstream, causing both the body and the brain to become undernourished. Many people in the Western world eat this bland, starchy, sugary food with the result that constipation is accepted as a normal part of life. Constipation, which is not often a problem among African and Asian people, can lead to diverticular disease, colitis, appendicitis, and many other major illnesses, including cancer of the colon.

To make matters worse, the better foods, like the vegetables and fruits so vital for life and health, are poorly cooked. The tender leaves and stems of fruits and vegetables are the most alkaline part of the plant, so they are best eaten raw and certainly not boiled to death as most British people think is necessary. When vegetables are cooked, it is best to lightly steam them so that they are left fairly crunchy. Always use the outer leaves of vegetables and lettuce for they are the best parts of the plant, containing most of the nutrients and particularly minerals. Better still, chop them up to make salads so full of fruits and vegetables of such colourful, tempting varieties that everyone, even to the most finicky child, will want to eat them. A glass of fresh raw juice can be added to make the meal even more healthy. Get into the habit of taking a glass of fruit juice on rising and last thing at night. To really feel the benefit of all this, alcohol and the usual beverages such as strong coffee and tea should be cut down or, better still, eliminated altogether.

Juices can be digested by children, by convalescents and by elderly people more easily than great amounts of raw food. Juices can be digested easily at any time of the day, even at bedtime. To get the same amount of nutrients as one gets from a pint of raw juice, one would have to eat plates of raw food. Raw juices have been used in many therapies to treat a variety of illnesses, as can be seen in the later chapters of this book, but juices are for everyone who wants to become more healthy and to stay healthy. They are also a highly palatable way of quenching your thirst at any time of day.

A good point to remember is that fruit juices stimulate the appetite and so are best taken in the mornings or before meals, in the conventional way. A refreshing glass of fruit juice taken to start the day will wake up the whole system. Vegetable juices, on the other hand, are generally slightly sedative and so can be taken quite safely in the evening for a sound night's sleep. Juices can be taken at any time of the day instead of temporarily-stimulating beverages such as tea, coffee or gassy drinks, and while their delicious aroma and delicate flavour are being savoured they will be doing a power of good as well.

The Historical Background

Raw juices have been used throughout history by physicians. The ancient Romans knew about the valuable goodness of juices and added them with herbs and honey to their drinks. Two centuries ago, German doctors gave onion juice to children to treat cases of worms. It was in the nineteenth century that the modern day pioneers of raw food and juice therapy started working, in an individual way, towards success in treating patients — and often themselves — with raw foods. People like Father Kniepp, Dr Kellogg and Dr Henry Lindlahr used the simplest methods in their cures — light, fresh air, raw food and exercise. Father Kniepp's treatment in Germany became famous and there is still a Kniepp Society in Germany. These pioneers saw that in successful healing the whole of the person had to be treated, not just a set of symptoms. We are now coming to accept this holistic outlook in treating disease and yet it was accepted by many people long ago. These early doctors realized that firstly the toxins in the body had to be expelled before there could be any success in fighting the disease. This had to be done by fasting and taking raw vegetable and fruit juices, and then continuing with a healthy diet of raw natural food.

The Swiss doctor, Max Bircher-Benner, was the founder of a famous clinic nearly a century ago which is still an authoratitive voice in the field of nutrition today. Bircher-Benner also took the holistic or 'whole person outlook' on healing. He is probably best known for his recipe for muesli, the now fashionable breakfast food, which he advocated soaking with fruit juice. Many other doctors have since followed this tradition of giving natural food and raw juices as a treatment for a variety of illnesses, and important clinics using such methods are still to be found in Germany.

Organically Grown Produce

Fruit and vegetables should be grown in organically rich soil. Organically grown produce is generally superior in flavour, quality, and nutritional value to fruit and vegetables grown with artificial chemical fertilizers and pesticides. When extracting health-giving juices then it is only sensible to get the best possible fruit and vegetables, or the end result will not be as healthy.

What is organically grown produce? It is anything grown in soil which has had only natural compost and other organic natural matter laid on it and has not been deeply dug, as this disturbs the subsoil. The compost's nutrients seep down into the soil with the action of the weather. The compost extracts plant food from tiny rock particles, something which chemical fertilizers cannot do. As well as giving important nourishment to the soil it can make poor soils more fertile by acting as a catalyst, unlocking many plant foods new to the soil. So while gardeners and farmers seem to do better with greater yields and profits when using chemicals, it is at the expense of the soil's fertility. Unless produce can be grown in one's own garden, or from a market garden known to grow its produce organically, then it must be assumed that all bought fruit and vegetables will not be organically grown. The produce may look as good or even better than organically grown products. There is, however, a lot of difference nutritionally — and some fruits may still have harmful sprays on them, so they must be washed thoroughly before using. Citrus fruits, for instance, have their life extended by the use of sprays and waxes on the fruit itself.

The only way to ensure that other British fruit and vegetables are organically grown is to produce them in the garden. It has been found that 100g of fresh garden carrots grown with artificial fertilizers contain only 0.5mg of carotene, which is converted into vitamin A by the body. In complete contrast, the same weight of carrots grown in compost-rich soil contains as much as 31mg of carotene — sixty-two times as much. Research has shown that organically grown foods usually have more vitamins, minerals and amino acids than those grown with artificial fertilizers. Plants grown on poor soils and fed with artificial fertilizers are generally lower in protein, minerals, vitamins and high in starches.

Types of Juice Extractors

Juice extractors must not be confused with electric blenders — they do quite different work. Juicers separate the juice from the pulp whereas the blender, also called a liquidizer, chops the food up into a creamy purée with no separation. There are two main types of extractor — one using direct pressure and the other using centrifugal force. The direct pressure method uses the basic lemon squeezer or garlic press. Juices made in this way are less likely to be oxidized during the process than by the centrifugal force type — but they are hardly labour-saving, especially if a large amount of juice is required. Nor are these types of juicers very efficient at getting all the juice out and some types of fruit and vegetables are not suitable as they have a low moisture content. On the other hand, centrifugal juice extractors can be used on all types of fresh produce. They shred the fruit and vegetable and then get the juice out by spinning at top speed. The juice passes through a fine sieve and the pulp is kept separate.

There are two types of centrifugal force juice extractor — the separator, the kind which does not have to be constantly cleared, and the batch type. The second type has to be cleared out after every two pounds of produce has been put through it. The separator type might be found to be more convenient as it expels, rather than fills up, with pulp. If a batch type is bought, go for an extractor with a large capacity which does not need emptying constantly. It will be a bad buy if, through having to empty it all the time for a family or when entertaining, the juicer becomes a nuisance and is eventually relegated to the back of the cupboard, instead of being used every day for good health.

The main drawback of the centrifugal type is that some air is mixed into the juice so oxidation can occur fairly soon and this reduces the vitamin value of the food. Therefore juice produced in this way should be used soon after processing. Citrus fruit has to be peeled for a centrifugal force type juicer, but specially designed citrus fruit juice extractors are now available. These take all the work out of processing these fruits — the halved fruit simply has to be pressed on to the central cone of the juicer and no peeling is required. As well as this, some juicers have citrus juice extractor attachments. This is very helpful if one has skin that is irritated by the peel and juice of citrus fruits.

Preparation of Fruit and Vegetables

Almost any type of fruit or vegetable can be made into juice. Try to buy or pick them as fresh as possible, again organically grown if possible, and do not store fresh food for long periods as this causes a loss of valuable vitamins. Fruit should be crisp and juicy. Do not use over-ripe or mushy fruit and cut away any brown spots on apples, pears, apricots and so on. Wash grapes and take them off the stems and remove the stones from fruit. Vegetables should be firm and free from discoloration. Cut away any brown marks from celery and root vegetables, but otherwise never peel them — and this goes for fruit as well — because so much of their goodness lies just beneath the skin. Just scrub them well and use the outer leaves, as these have the most minerals. The golden rule is never to use inferior produce but always the best quality you can obtain. Smaller pieces of fruit and vegetables usually contain more nutrients than the larger chunks. This is probably because they have a larger proportion of skin in relation to their flesh. Therefore cut all produce up into small pieces for the juicer. A little lemon juice can be added to apple juice and to celery juice to prevent discoloration.

Fresh juices should not come into contact with any metal except stainless steel, or a chemical reaction may set in, especially with aluminium or tin. For the same reason use only bowls and jars made from plastic, glass, china, enamel or earthenware. When you have made your juice, add some ice to its storage container. This will help to reduce oxidation. Although juice is best drunk straight away, it can be stored in the fridge for a few hours in an airtight container or a flask, with some ice. But, generally, it must never be frozen or the vital enzymes and goodness in the juice will be destroyed. Another idea is to pour a little olive oil on to the top of the jar containing the juice, which will then spread evenly over the top and form an airtight film. If you use a wide-mouthed jar with a screw-top, a hole can be made in each side of the lid and the oil can be poured off — leaving the juice behind.

1

Fruit Juices

Apple Juice

There is probably less vitamin C in apples than was once thought — and certainly less than in citrus fruits — but they are still invaluable for a good healthy feeling of vitality as they contain many other vitamins and minerals. Apple juice is also so delicious that it will be a firm favourite, especially with children, and it is easily digested.

Freshly-extracted apple juice contains large amounts of carotene (which converts to vitamin A), many of the B complex of vitamins, vitamins C and P, as well as biotin and pantothenic acid. There is a high proportion of pectin, malic acid and tannic acid in apples; these help to purify the blood, clean out the liver and keep the skin feeling fresh and youthful. The acids help the digestion, contrary to what a lot of people think, as they make the stomach juices work more efficiently.

The mineral content of apples is extremely high, including calcium, phosphorus, iron, magnesium, potassium, sodium chloride and sulphur. Some apples have more vitamin C than others. *Cox's* and *Jonathans*, *Bramleys* and *Beauty of*

Bath have the most, while *Laxton's Superb, James Grieve*
and *Rome Beauty* have the least amounts; somewhere in
between come *Golden Delicious* and *Worcester Pairmain.* The
vitamin C content helps to prevent and fight off infections
of the intestine. It also improves the appetite and it protects
the blood vessels, lymphatic tubes and other cavities. It is
essential for the glands to work properly. Vitamin A works
alongside vitamin C in fighting stomach and intestinal
infections. While we realize that we must have vitamin A
for our health, it is not always understood that the vitamin
stimulates the secretions which lubricate the mucous
membranes throughout the body. The B complex vitamins
stimulate the appetite and help the other foods we eat to
be digested and assimilated by the body. We must have B
vitamins for healthy nerve tissues and cells. Malic acid is
an excellent disinfectant for the stomach and intestines. It
helps treat catarrh, poor appetite, liver disorders, kidney
complaints and general under-nourishment.

Apple juice is good for treating diarrhoea and bowel
complaints so it is extremely good to give to young children
and babies with bowel problems. Slowly-cooked, unsweetened
apple purée has a high pectin value. This makes it mildly
laxative and if taken at breakfast will establish easy bowel
movements every day. In this way all forms of laxatives can
be avoided — and while the child is having an enjoyable
drink. In fact, constipation is the scourge of modern times,
a combination of over-refined foods and rushed, often
stressful, lives. But constipation can lead to more serious
illnesses, such as colitis, diverticular disease, appendicitis,
and even cancer of the colon. Eating fresh fruit and drinking
raw vegetable or fruit juice each day will give the fibre, the
vitamins and minerals needed to keep the bowels normally
active. With these nutrients we feel energetic and well;

without them we feel the sluggishness and lack of vitality that goes with constipation. Commercial laxatives are not the answer for children, nor are they the answer for adults. Millions of pounds are spent on them each year, yet by keeping to a good well-balanced diet with plenty of fibre there is no need at all for any laxatives. Freshly-pressed apple juice has been called Nature's greatest regulator, for it keeps the intestines toned-up with smooth, natural movements. It makes the body resistant to many infections and, as it prevents constipation, it stops harmful bacteria building up in the intestinal tract as well.

Apples contain about ten calories per ounce. When juicing them, do not put the core into the juicer as some people are upset by the substance contained in the pips.

The following are recipes for some 'apple cocktails':

Combine apple juice and carrot juice in equal amounts of, for instance, eight fluid ounces.

To six fluid ounces of carrot juice, add five fluid ounces each of celery and apple juices.

To six fluid ounces of apple juice, add eight fluid ounces of carrot juice and just two fluid ounces of spinach juice.

This is something rather special — perhaps for a party. Press between four and six cups of apple juice, add two teaspoonsful of honey, a lemon or an orange (both if you wish), half a dozen cloves, four cinnamon sticks, two cardamom pods, a pinch of nutmeg, allspice and ground cinnamon. Cut the lemon and orange into thin slices and place in a jug. Pour the apple juice over them, then add the honey and spices, but not the cinnamon sticks. Cover and leave to stand for an hour. Strain the juice and serve in glasses with a stick of cinnamon in each.

Apricot Juice

High in vitamin A and iron, apricots are good for the mucous membranes and respiratory organs and they are marvellous cleansers for the whole body. Apricots are highly alkaline and are excellent for conditions in which there has been a build-up of too much acid in the body. They are valuable for people suffering with anaemia, impure blood, asthma, catarrh, diarrhoea and gallstones. As well as vitamin A apricots contain vitamin B_6, at least six minerals including potassium, iron, pantothenic acid and folic acid, plus other essential vitamins.

The perfect apricot will only keep for a day if you are buying fresh ones, so select only ripe but good quality fruit and use the juice immediately or freeze it. Besides being a delightful juice, this is one of the best ways to eat apricots. So often people only buy them for bottling and jam-making; this is a great shame, for so many of the nutrients in apricots are lost in the cooking process, with refined white sugar and the addition of chemicals such as sulphur dioxide.

Cherry Juice

Cherry juice is good for people with gout and arthritis. It is useful for controlling uric acid in the body.

The stones should be taken out and the stalks removed from the cherries before juicing.

Grape Juice

Grape juice diets have been famous throughout Europe for many years. Unhealthy and overweight Europeans flocked to resorts in northern Italy, Austria and southern Germany to take the grape-cure during harvest-time — and have a good holiday as well. The lucky people lazed around and sipped only grape juice for several weeks, increasing the amounts from three to eight pounds daily according to their age and strength. This cure is especially helpful for anaemic conditions and for disease of the respiratory tract and the kidneys. It is successful because the juice gives protein and carbohydrate in its most easily-assimilated form. The large proportion of alkaline salts such as potash, lime, magnesia and iron reduce the blood's acidity. Grape juice helps to cut down weight, as it burns up fat. Although it has a high sugar content, this is readily absorbed by the body. People can also exist on grape juice as it is a source of quick energy to the body, being so quickly converted into nutrients. So the grape cure really is a good idea; as it is so easily and quickly used in the body, it can be taken by people with low blood sugar (or hypoglycaemia) problems.

Fresh grape juice contains vitamins A, B and C — but these are partly lost when the juice is pasteurized or preserved. So, although there are many grape juices on the market, it really is best to make your own. Grape juice is one of the richest sources of organic iron. It reduces over-acidity, fights off blood disorders, especially anaemia, poor circulation, skin disorders, liver trouble, nervous exhaustion, rheumatism, arthritis, digestive disorders, low blood-pressure, inflammation of the mouth and pyorrhoea (gum disease).

Grapefruit Juice

It may surprise you to learn that grapefruit juice contains almost as much fruit sugar as orange juice. It is also rich in vitamin C. With good reason it is popular as a breakfast food and as a starter in menus, for its slightly bitter taste stimulates the flow of stomach juices and the appetite. In the morning grapefruit juice moves the bowels and so helps to overcome constipation, especially if taken in a regime of natural foods. Anyone suffering from high blood-pressure, sluggish liver, gall stones, arthritis, obesity, ailments of the respiratory tract and digestive disturbances, should take grapefruit juice. On the other hand, if you are a sufferer of colitis, and stomach or duodenal ulcers, you should not take grapefruit juice as it is too high in citric acid.

As with all citrus juices, dilute grapefruit juice with water and sweeten with a little honey. Be careful not to take concentrated citrus juices at any time except before a meal or the citric acid may interfere with the calcium balance in the body which may cause tooth decay. But you should not suffer from this if you dilute the juice or take it and then eat straight away.

Lemon Juice

The essential oils in lemons are very good for cooling the body temperature so it is an excellent drink if you have a fever, either caused by illness or too much sun. This is why lemonade is so refreshing and why it has been taken in hot climates, for centuries, and even in our cooler climes when the sun does beat down. Because of its high vitamin C content lemon juice was used by sailors taking long sea journeys to ward off scurvy. Lemons contain a good deal of calcium but not much sodium and therefore lemon juice is also a useful flavouring in a low-salt diet.

It is wise to wash the skin of the fruit because sometimes the keeping qualities and the appearance have been improved by the use of chemicals and by waxing. Be sure to choose firm clear-skinned fruit for juicing, with no deterioration near the stem mark at the top of the lemon. The pulp that will be left over from juicing lemons need not be wasted: it is marvellous for the skin and can help to soothe insect bites and stings. Just add equal parts of toilet water, glycerine and pulp and the mixture will make a good — and cheap — hand cream.

Lemon juice kills off bacteria very quickly and some doctors have found that within fifteen minutes it can kill nearly all the bacteria present in raw oysters, (although of course that does leave a small amount behind which may be toxic). When it is vapourized, lemon juice can also kill off the harmful bacteria causing typhoid, meningitis, and pneumonia within an hour and a half. So for any impending illness, always take some lemon juice to kill the bacteria quickly and reduce the temperature. A lemon is a most beneficial fruit for use as a general tonic and especially for the respiratory tract.

Orange Juice
Probably the most popular fruit juice around, orange juice is at its most nutritious when freshly pressed. It is full of vitamin C, which must be replaced in the body every day, and therefore it is most valuable in the winter months as a guard against illness. There are between 50 and 100mg of vitamin C in 100g of the fruit. There are also plenty of bioflavonoids, or vitamin P, in oranges; these are the substances that make the orange so much more beneficial than some other fruits as they work in conjunction with the vitamins. Also called rutin and hesperidin, they are used in concentrated form to treat high blood-pressure and in treating colds. For more of this, see the section on bioflavonoids (page 65). Oranges also contain a small amount of minerals.

Oranges have a laxative quality, and if fresh orange juice is taken both last thing at night and again on rising a routine of normal bowel movements will be established thus eliminating any problems of constipation.

Papaya Juice

Try to find this exotic fruit, for it is an extremely rich source of proteolytic enzymes. These are the chemicals that make it possible to digest the protein in the diet. The most important of these enzymes is called the papain; it is extracted and used as a powder to help digestion and also as a meat-tenderizer.

It has been claimed by many experts that the papaya possesses rejuvenating qualities and that it can prevent early ageing. People who have difficulty in digesting food have found that papaya works better than anything else and that is has been the major factor in their return to health. There is little fat but some protein in the fruit and also very high levels of vitamin A and C, which work best in combination. Its other enzymes are arginine, known to be important in maintaining fertility levels in men, and carpain, which is believed to be beneficial for the heart. There is also a rare substance called fibrin in the papaya fruit which is thought to be important in blood clotting. So hunt for it — the best place to track down the papaya would be in shops run by the West Indian and Indian communities.

Peach Juice

That most succulent fruit, the peach, contains large amounts of vitamins A and C, as well as thiamin, riboflavin, niacin, and a whole list of other nutrients including calcium, iron, phosphorus, copper, manganese, chlorine, inositol, and pantothenic acid. When juicing peaches do not discard any left-over pulp, because it contains much fibre which is useful for those suffering with constipation or other bowel problems. It is especially good for treating colitis.

It is recommended that peaches should be peeled unless it is positively known that they have not been sprayed with insecticides, as it is extremely difficult to wash off sprays from such a furry skin. Although they contain malic, tartaric and citric acid, peaches, like most other fruits, produce an alkaline reaction in the body.

Pear Juice
Helpful for people with digestive disorders and constipation, pears make a delicious fruit juice. They contain less acid than almost any other fruit. They should be used only when they are fully ripe, when they are at their best, for they do start to go 'off' very quickly and then their nutritious value is lost.

Plum Juice
Plums contain large amounts of A and B vitamins, some quantities of vitamin P as well as calcium, phosphorus, copper and manganese. The fruit also contains benzoic acid and fruit sugars. Plum juice helps the digestion and can be used to regulate the bowels. As it makes the urine acid it is unsuitable for people on a strictly alkaline diet, but for most people this acid-forming process does not matter.

Prune Juice
Prunes are simply dried plums of a certain variety. They are allowed to ripen fully on the tree and fall to the ground before drying. Their nutritional content is the same as that of plums except that they can be stored for far longer once they have been dried. Do take care not to buy prunes treated with sulphur or other chemicals when they were dried, as this will probably mean that their nutritional value is lower.

Pumpkin Juice
The Pilgrim Fathers prepared themselves well for the winter

when they added pumpkin pie to their Thanksgiving dinner and made it a traditional part of the feast, for it is a rich source of vitamin C and so a very good food to eat in the dark months. The pumpkin is related to the squash and the courgette. Its seeds are very valuable; they have been used to help the prostate gland work properly in older men and to preserve virility. In fact, the peasants in the Balkans have been taking pumpkin seeds for centuries for those reasons. Pumpkin seeds are rich in iron and phosphorus and are a good source of vitamin B, vitamin A and calcium. They contain thirty per cent protein and forty per cent fat which is rich in unsaturated fatty acids. The pumpkin is used for the treatment of tapeworms, helping to remove them from the digestive tract. The kidneys are gently worked by the juice and water retention is reduced, leaving the urine normal and without unpleasant side-effects.

Pineapple Juice

Like apples, pineapples vary in their vitamin C content — from 24 to 165mg in every 100g. If they are canned or bottled, this value is cut by about a third. So if you can, buy fresh fruit. It is best to choose ripe fruit with a good deep colour — green pineapples do not get any sweeter with storage nor does their nutritional value improve. Pineapples need to be picked when they are fully mature because it is only in the final stage of ripening that the starch in the stem is taken up into the fruit and converted to sugar.

It is when the pineapple is at its sweetest that it will give you most benefit. It will relieve sore throats and bronchitis, so it is just as well that it is readily available in the wintertime. For more serious illness, pineapples are good for the heart as the fruit reduces the time taken to coagulate the blood; but for this reason the fruit should not be taken by people with diseases of the kidney or liver or who suffer with haemophilia. When tuberculosis was a scourge the juice was found to be good in dissolving mucus and helping the patient back to good health. Pineapples have also been recommended to many women for the treatment of painful periods. The juice is good for the glands and helps to regulate them. It also has a mildly diuretic effect and may be taken by people suffering with croup and tonsillitis and in cases where protein foods cause digestive upsets. Pineapple juice has even been recommended for motorists, to help them see alertly at night on long-distance drives.

Rhubarb Juice

Rhubarb is generally regarded as a treatment for constipation and diarrhoea. On the other hand it should be used sparingly because of its high oxalic acid content which combines with calcium to form crystals of insoluble calcium oxalate that cannot be used by the body. Rhubarb is very rich in calcium but because of its acid content this cannot be used by the body.

Strawberry Juice

When strawberries are made into preserves much of their high vitamin C content is lost, so they should be eaten raw or juiced. Strawberries also contain vitamin A, thiamin, riboflavin, niacin, pyridoxine, pantothenic acid, biotin, calcium, phosphorus and iron. Their calcium and iron content is higher than many fruits and half a cupful of strawberries is the equivalent in vitamin C to an orange. Thus they are a very valuable fruit and should not be just kept for special occasions. Strawberry juice is good for people with anaemia and has been used in the treatment of other illness, including pellagra and sprue.

Strawberries must be used as quickly as possible after picking as their vitamin content is soon lost. They should be kept in the fridge if there is a need to store them.

2

Vegetable Juices

Alfalfa Juice
It is extremely easy to sprout alfalfa in a jam-jar or bean-sprouter, as it grows as rapidly as mustard and cress. It is an invaluable source of vitamins and minerals, especially in the winter months when vegetables are getting old and have lost much of their food value because of long-term storage. Alfalfa contains very high amounts of vitamin A and vitamin C. It has extremely long roots which go deep down into the soil — sometimes to a depth of one hundred and twenty feet — gathering strength from many trace elements. There is a rich and balanced amount of calcium, magnesium, phosphorus, chlorine, sodium, potassium and silicon as a result. Alfalfa also contains one of the lesser known vitamins — K. This is also found in yogurt, kelp, green vegetables, egg yolks, and some oils — soyabean, safflower, and fish-liver oils. Excessive diarrhoea is a pointer that there is a vitamin K deficiency. The vitamin helps the blood to clot properly, and it is particularly useful in reducing heavy menstrual flow, and in preventing internal bleeding and haemorrhages.

Alfalfa juice has also been used to treat heart and artery problems with great success. This is thought to be because excessive gas can build up in the colon, pressing the walls of the colon against the heart and arteries. When the plant is juiced, only the leaves are used. It is too strong and powerful to be taken on its own, but is excellent with carrot juice.

Artichoke Juice

The properties of the artichoke have been well known in parts of Europe for many centuries. In Italy, France and Germany it forms the basis for many drinks when fortified by alcohol. The artichoke is very rich in calcium and contains some valuable oils which help to stabilize the metabolism. It can also help liver complaints and is a most useful diuretic that can be taken by people who have problems with water retention.

This is a useful recipe for 'artichoke elixir':

Make 2 oz of artichoke leaves into juice, then add both the juice and the pulp that is left over to a bottle of white wine. Leave it for a week, then strain into a clean bottle.

Start drinking it straight away — a wineglassful each day is the correct dosage. It is a great help to store artichoke juice in this way because it will keep for a very long time and artichokes are not always available or cheap. When buying artichokes, look for a good colour, well-closed leaves in the centre of the 'choke' and make sure there are not any bruises or blemishes. The base should not look woody.

Asparagus Juice

Like artichokes, asparagus is a luxury item on the shopping list but well worth the money for it contains much vitamin

C, folic acid and potassium. Although present only in tiny quantities there are also some powerful essential oils. It is possible to grow asparagus in the garden and so save expense; it is still grown wild in the Mediterranean areas. The old name for it is 'sparrow grass' and farmers still call it grass.

In the asparagus plant is a substance called the alkaloid asparagine which has a rapid effect on the kidneys, making them work quicker within hours of taking the plant either as a food or a juice. It is therefore excellent as a diuretic for treating the kidneys. The urine which results has a strong colour and smell, but this is not a cause for alarm. When drinking asparagus juice, do not take too much because it is so powerful — a sherry glassful is enough.

It is best to buy asparagus with fresh-looking stems, not dried out; the thickness of the stems does not matter. The white, woody base of the stem helps to stop the asparagus from drying out, so wrap it in a damp cloth and keep it for a few days in a cool place, ideally the vegetable drawer of the fridge.

Avocado Juice

Many of us fight shy of the avocado because, although we find it delicious, we know it is high in calories and therefore we think of it just as something rather fattening. This is a pity because for all that it is 165 calories for every 100g, it is packed with goodness. There are eleven vitamins and seventeen minerals, a very good supply of carotene which is converted into vitamin A, and a high level of oil in the avocado. The oil contains A, D and E and it is second only to lanolin in being the most penetrating oil that the human skin can absorb. Unlike lanolin, which causes allergies in many people, oil of avocado is allergy-free and quite safe to use. It is the perfect treatment for sensitive skins.

It is best to buy ripe avocado pears, or at least ripen them before using them, for there is three times as much carotene in a fully-ripened avocado as in a hard one. There has been a scare in recent years about the supposed toxic qualities of avocado pears. It is true that some animals have been somewhat affected in this way but there is no evidence that there is any danger to human beings. However, to be on the safe side, it is advised that people eat no more than one avocado a day, either fresh or as juice.

Beetroot Juice

Much has been written about the medicinal powers of beetroot juice, particularly in the treatment of cancer. In France there have been many experiments concerning the use of large quantities of the juice — up to seven pints a day — to help cancer patients. There have been some good results but research still has a long way to go before it can be conclusively proved that beetroot juice kills cancerous growths. In Germany, beetroot juice is a popular tonic for restoring health through convalescence. A Hungarian doctor, Dr S. Firenczi, started giving beetroot juice therapy treatment to cancer patients at his clinic nearly thirty-five years ago. He had good results in fifteen out of sixteen cases with the tumours definitely reduced, the patients gaining weight and their blood count showing signs of great improvement. For more details see the chapter on beetroot therapy. Even the Greeks of ancient times believed that beetroot was good for cooling the blood and the Romans used it to treat feverish illnesses, especially among children.

The iron content in beetroot is not very high but it is present in a form that is easy to digest. Beetroot is high in amino acids and minerals — phosphorus, sodium, calcium, potassium and magnesium. We also know that beetroot is good for regulating the digestive system. It is high in easily-digested carbohydrates, but cooking it reduces the vitamin content, so it is best juiced raw.

Brussels Sprout Juice

Although the Brussels sprout is one of our best sources of vitamin C in winter, it is easy to see that in many British households most of that goodness is lost. If Brussels sprouts are not eaten raw, and they can be chopped up in salads just like any other vegetable, they should be gently steamed for a few minutes. Instead, too many people just boil and boil them until they are like limp yellow rags, all the green colour and vitamins having been transferred to the cooking water which usually ends up being poured down the sink. A cup of Brussels sprouts weighing 100g gives 100mg of vitamin C, but when they are boiled the vitamin C content goes down to 35mg.

The juice of the Brussels sprout is combined with runner or string bean juice as a treatment for diabetes, in adults. The children's type of diabetes is the more severe and they must have insulin injections, but adults can often be treated with diet, tablets or raw juice therapy. Treatment should always be supervised for the individual patient by a fully-qualified practitioner.

Cabbage Juice

The cabbage is thought to be one of the first vegetables cultivated by man. Indeed, this valuable source of goodness has long been an aid to good health. For a considerable number of years it has been the subject of research. The cabbage has a complex structure scientifically, and there have been a wide variety of studies on the vegetable. It is still not fully known which are the exact properties of the cabbage that do so much good; but the factor that is believed to have been responsible for great success in the treatment of gastric ulcers has been called vitamin U. This vitamin has a similar make-up to vitamin K. It is easily destroyed by heat and by oxidation. It is also killed by exposure to light and air. A deficiency of vitamin U may be caused by poor diet or due to a defect of the metabolism such as a liver malfunction.

Cabbage juice can treat infections, ulcers and other digestive disorders. When cabbage is concentrated into juice it is just as effective and great success has been recorded in the case of patients who took cabbage juice for their complaints. One point should be made about cabbage juice. Neither the juice nor the complete vegetable should be taken in excess, i.e., so that it becomes the main part of the diet. This can result in enlarged goitre, which is a disease of the thyroid gland. However, if the vegetable or the juice are taken in normal amounts, this should not happen. It is not a pleasant drink, in any case, so that should not make it tempting to take in large quantities.

Several tests have been carried out on ulcer patients using cabbage juice. In one, a hundred patients were given the juice for several days and by the fifth day pain had gone. Except in the most serious cases, the patient was healed within fourteen days whereas the usual time for healing is about seven weeks. The patients took 16 fl oz or 450ml of cabbage juice in regular small amounts. Out of a hundred patients, only five did not show improvement. In another test, eighty-one patients with ulcers of varying degrees were treated with cabbage juice. There were forty-three cases with small ulcers, twenty-eight with large ulcers, and ten had ulcers of a huge size. The ulcers were measured and their sizes noted. The daily dose for the treatment was one quart of juice, given in divided doses. The concentrate given to the majority of the patients was taken from between one and two quarts of freshly-pressed cabbage juice. The capsules were the equivalent of a daily amount of 100g of whole raw cabbage. A complete case-history was built up on each patient and everyone was re-examined with X-rays of other organs at intervals throughout the treatment and, where possible, for between three and six months after starting the therapy. As well as testing the urine, blood and stools of each patient, most of them also had a gastric analysis. For twenty-eight patients there were at least two uropepsin tests, and a dozen had a gastroscopic examination. Other tests included those on the pancreas and the liver, and there were gastric washes to seek out any possible tumours. A small group of patients could not be followed through to a final analysis: either because they did not return for enough follow-up tests; or because they were forced to have an operation by other doctors; and some of whom had cancer of the stomach diagnosed. Another two patients died from heart disease — one of them, an elderly woman, died suddenly of an attack only eight days after starting the therapy. The other, an eighty year old man, was showing improvement while receiving therapy, but developed acute cardiac failure and died.

Only three people, of the patients who carried through with the treatment, still had unhealed ulcers by the end of the tests. These were cases which were far more complicated than the others. One had complications surrounding a huge ulcer which penetrated into the pancreas. A second had long-standing chronic hepatitis and recent active hepatitis during the time of treatment on his large gastric ulcer. When there was no sign of healing after three weeks of juice therapy, exploratory surgery showed a large benign gastric ulcer and a biopsy on the liver showed that hepatitis was markedly active. The third case was a woman who had a constantly recurring ulcer niche at the outlet of the stomach. Although healing was noted for periods during the course of treatment, it was not consistent.

The small ulcers healed on average within about a fortnight, larger ulcers taking seven or ten days longer to heal. The patients with huge ulcers, the sort that are usually operated on during orthodox treatment, in some cases showed healing after just over two months. As some patients kept fairly active during the juice therapy but did not respond so well as those on bed-rest, and in fact recovered when given bed-rest, it was recommended that bed-rest be a part of the treatment of large gastric ulcers.

The conclusions at the end of the tests showed that there is a strong case for giving cabbage juice therapy to sufferers of gastric ulcers before considering surgery. Benign gastric ulcers of all sizes all tend to heal completely and quite quickly when this sort of therapy is given. It would be better if people could take cabbage juice regularly, as a preventative measure, rather than having to go through the pain of an ulcer and then seeking treatment which can take quite a time before the ulcer heals itself.

Carrot Juice

Carrot juice is one of the finest natural medicines available to us. It has been known as a medicine ever since ancient times and it is certainly one of the best-flavoured vegetable juices. It is the richest source of carotene, which is the reason for its yellow colour. Carotene is converted into vitamin A by our bodies. Other sources of the vitamin are eggs and butter, which have the disadvantage of being high in cholesterol and bad for the heart and arteries if taken in fairly large quantities — as many people still do. Carrots also contain an ample supply of the other vitamins — B, C, D, E, G and K, as well as the minerals potassium, sodium, calcium, magnesium, sulphur, copper, and chlorine. Choose strongly coloured carrots, not the very pale types. Early ones are usually paler than the more mature vegetables, and these early carrots are low in carotene.

If children will not eat carrots they may be persuaded to drink carrot juice instead, which will probably do them more good than boiled-away-to-nothing cooked carrots. Nursing mothers are told to take carrot juice to improve the quality of their milk. It is a good idea to start taking carrot juice during pregnancy to give the baby a fine source of nutrition.

Carrots are believed to be good for strengthening the eyes — hence the legend of the wartime bomber crews being given carrots to guard against night-blindness. This condition is also called glare-blindness and its symptoms are difficulty in adjusting sight in a dim light, such as going into a dark room or theatre from a brightly-lit hall. This type of eye defect is more serious when a motorist is unable to adjust focus after seeing the glare of oncoming car headlights. This has led to many serious road accidents.

We need vitamin A for healthy mucous membranes which line all the body cavities. These membranes are made up of two layers, the top layer or epithelium, which has billions of cells, and underneath the mucous membrane itself, a thin layer of muscle fibres. These are very pliable and elastic, and the quality of this lining depends on it getting enough vitamin A. Without sufficient vitamin A the cells harden into a rough surface and this blocks the secretion of the mucus which acts as a disinfectant. Lack of the vitamin results in infections of the mouth, tonsils, sinuses, tongue, ear, eyes, bladder, kidneys or the alimentary tract. Apart from building up a resistance to a variety of infections, vitamin A also keeps the body tissues healthy and strong, keeps the glands functioning well, and promotes the growth of bones and teeth. Signs of a deficiency are dry, scaly skin, intestinal disorders and diarrhoea, poor appetite, lack of growth and vitality, weight-loss and weakness, poor teeth and gums, and atrophy of the glands. Nerves may be affected and there may be kidney or bladder stones. It is thought to be the cause of some cases of infertility. Be careful not to use mineral oil as a food dressing as it has the effect of carrying off the vitamin before it has been absorbed by the system. This type of oil should only be used temporarily when necessary and then only on the advice of a physician.

Tissues become diseased when the natural protection against bacteria of vitamin A is not available to the body. By taking a daily supply of the vitamin, infections should be held at bay. Where a deficiency has been found it can be caused by either not taking enough vitamin A or by a faulty metabolism. This does need medical help and should not be left to the individual for self-diagnosis and treatment. The minimum amounts of vitamin A needed for good health, as given out in this country, vary from 1,500 IU (international units) for babies under one year to 5,000 IU for adults. Children up to twelve years need between 2,000 and 3,500 IU while for teenage girls it rises to 4,500-5,000, and for teenage boys between 4,500 and 6,000. Nursing mothers require the highest amounts of the vitamin daily — 8,000 IU. Pregnant women need 6,000 IU. These are only the minimum requirements however, and more is needed for really good health.

Nearly all our vitamin A is stored in the liver. Smaller amounts are found in the kidneys, lungs and under the skin. The liver can store large amounts of vitamin A for years, keeping it for when it is needed. It is important to keep 'topping-up' this store and not to let it run down. An eight-ounce glass of fresh carrot juice will give, on average, 50,000 IU of vitamin A. This is the best way of absorbing the vitamin and gives the most nutrients to the body and, more than just meeting the daily minimum, it provides a good surplus which can be stored for any future need. While it is possible to take too much vitamin A as it is stored in the body, one would have to take pounds of carrots each and every day for this to happen.

Another vitamin contained in carrot juice is vitamin E; this has been attributed with many qualities in the past, including that of improving sexual performance. In tests on animals the vitamin has been found to affect reproduction and sterility levels — which is rather different. A link has been found between vitamin E and cancer. In one test, when a blood serum lacking vitamin E was used, the cancer cells increased rapidly. When cancer tissue was placed in a blood serum enriched with vitamin E, the cancer cells did not grow.

Carrot tops are also a source of goodness, rich in vitamin K, magnesium and chlorophyll. So they should not be thrown away but added to soups, shredded into salads or steamed lightly as a green vegetable.

Celery Juice

Celery's most important quality is its essential oils and concentrations of plant hormones. These oils have a specific effect on the regulation of the nervous system and produce a great calming effect. Celery has a long medical history. The ancient Greeks knew of its value and in medieval times celery was taken for disorders of the liver and gall bladder, for stones in the bladder and kidneys, for constipation and for menstrual problems. It has a good balance of vitamins and other nutrients, including the minerals, chlorides, potassium and sodium. The oils are found in the seeds as well as in the main part of the plant.

Celery has been used to bring a weak sexual system back to normality, and its strong diuretic effect makes it a good treatment for arthritis and rheumatism. If it is taken as a juice it is of most benefit. Add a tablespoonful of honey to celery juice and sip it slowly. For those on diets celery juice will help to reduce the appetite or it can be taken as a bedtime drink because, like most vegetables, it has a soothing, sedative effect.

Comfrey Juice

The country name for comfrey is 'knitbone' and for centuries it has been used as a healing herb for wounds, and as a cure for ulcers. Comfrey is one of the very few plants to contain vitamin B_{12}, which prevents anaemia. Vegetarians and particularly vegans, who do not eat dairy products, are at risk of becoming deficient in this important vitamin and so this is an important plant source for them. Vitamin B_{12} can be stored in the body for several years so if a person changes from a dairy, and perhaps meat-based, diet to a vegan one the deficiency may not be apparent until the onset of illness.

The active part of the plant is called allantoin which is believed to be a healing agent stimulating healthy tissue formation. It has been used in the treatment of gastric ulcers and in some skin preparations.

When juicing comfrey leaves, it is possible to use the roots as well if the plant is young.

Cucumber Juice

Cucumber is low in calories but a good source of potassium and vitamins, and has for centuries been known as a marvellous skin tonic. Like celery and carrot juice, it is also well known for treating rheumatic conditions. Cucumber is perhaps the best diuretic, stimulating the urine, and so is an invaluable treatment for water retention. Also, because it has a high amount of silicon and sulphur, it is a good hair tonic, especially when it is mixed with carrot, lettuce and spinach juice. It helps prevent hair from falling out — and it will help stop nails splitting. Its high potassium content makes the juice of the cucumber very valuable in the treatment of high or low blood-pressure. It can, too, help dental problems of both teeth and gums, especially pyorrhoea.

All in all, cucumber juice is a first-rate beauty treatment, helping the skin, nails, hair as well as encouraging the body to function efficiently. Add some carrot and lettuce juice, for skin complaints, and perhaps a little alfalfa to speed up the process. The whole of the cucumber, peel as well, can be used when juicing. Wash it well first, as it is highly likely that it will have been sprayed, unless it is from an organic source.

Dandelion Juice

The French word for this humble plant is 'Pissenlit' which means 'wet the bed' — and that gives the clue to its diuretic qualities. But is is a wonder-worker in so many ways, with an abundance of iron (almost as much as spinach), rich supplies of magnesium, vitamin A, potassium, calcium and sodium.

Dandelions are grown as a crop in some countries, particularly Belgium. Apart from being used as a salad vegetable when the plant is young, dandelions are also extensively grown and roasted into a coffee substitute; this has none of the harmful, stimulating qualities of caffeine, but instead is good for the digestion and for rheumatic complaints.

Magnesium, contained in dandelion juice, is essential for firming up the bones. If a pregnant woman takes enough magnesium and calcium, the growing baby's bones will develop strongly and the woman will not have dental problems caused by the baby taking too much calcium from her own supply. We need magnesium in a balanced combination with calcium, iron and sulphur for good blood formation. Magnesium gives us vitality and builds up the blood cells, especially those of the tissues of the lungs and the nervous system. Organic magnesium can only be obtained from live fresh plants and must be used fresh or raw. It is best not to use inorganic manufactured magnesium as this will only interfere with the working of the body. Chemically-produced magnesium produces only temporary results and can have bad after-effects on the body. Deposits build up in the system and cause damage, whereas fresh organic magnesium has the reverse effect.

Use raw dandelion leaves and roots and mix with carrot and turnips for a juice that will help spinal and other bone ailments, as well as making the teeth healthy and strong.

Fennel Juice

Fennel is a vegetable that can be used in a variety of ways; from its flavour it can be guessed that with its aniseed taste it is the base for liquorice and brandy-based drinks. Fennel leaves are a decorative addition to any herb garden. The root, which can be eaten raw or cooked, is similar to celery, but it has an essential oil that makes it special.

Fennel juice is used to treat night-blindness and other eye complaints, when combined with carrot juice. Beetroot juice mixed with fennel and carrot juice is an excellent remedy for anaemia, especially the sort that results from heavy periods. The French use fennel juice for migraine headaches.

It is considered a good general tonic to clean out the system, with its high level of vitamins C, A and B complex, and many minerals including sulphur, calcium, iron, phosphorus and potassium. Fennel juice can also be taken for indigestion and to help people recover from any illness.

French or String Bean Juice

French bean juice is used for convalescents and to treat gout, in fairly small quantities of about half a glass (5 fl oz); diabetics need more. It is usually taken in combination with Brussels sprout juice as a nervous stimulant and it is believed by some practitioners that it stimulates the body's insulin production. But, of course, any treatment should be under the control of a qualified practitioner.

While containing a variety of vitamins and minerals, the French or string bean is not very high in any one constituent but possesses a good overall balance to make it a very worthwhile juice to take.

Garlic Juice

So much has been written about garlic, since early times, that it has become something of a legend. Today it is becoming accepted as a part of good cooking in this country, as we become more cosmopolitan.

Garlic is nature's great disinfectant: used in medical treatment to clean wounds; always throughout history it has been taken as a cure-all; now, especially, it is used to treat colds and catarrh. Like onion juice, a dessertspoonful in half a pint of warm water is a well-tried remedy for treating worms in children. People with intestinal complaints have been treated with garlic with great success, as have tuberculosis sufferers. The list of illnesses and ailments that have been helped by garlic goes on and on — from bronchitis to amoebic dysentery, from asthma to arteriosclerosis. It can help reduce high blood-pressure and centuries ago it protected people from the plague.

It is not easy to extract juice from garlic. The cloves have to be crushed to preserve the essential oils which are its chief value. The liquid that is gained from crushing is added to other juices or it can be taken in small amounts by itself. The smell of garlic juice is even stronger than garlic used in cooking. It is these essential oils that help to dissolve the build-up of mucus in the sinus cavities, in the bronchial tubes and in the lungs. As well as cleansing the intestines from poisons garlic is also a strong diuretic — but be warned, the process can be rather sudden and dramatic.

If the heavy aroma of garlic and its anti-social effects are really disliked, then it can be taken in garlic perle forms. These days there are several types which are completely odourless and, if taken regularly, they should give almost as much protection as the juice.

Horseradish Juice

While this is a wonderful herb for treating mucus in the nose and the sinuses, it is also extremely powerful to take. The essential oils in the plant are so concentrated that it is really too strong to take as a juice, so instead it is usually taken as horseradish sauce. The sauce is made by shredding and pounding the root and adding lemon juice to it. This can be stored for up to a week in the fridge or a cold place. Take it undiluted in the morning and afternoon, just half a teaspoon. It does produce a reaction of headiness, sometimes accompanied by sweating. If that is extremely offputting, it is only fair to say that it does go straight to the cause of sinus trouble and bring relief. Sometimes it is necessary to take the horseradish sauce for several months and it is good to combine it with the juice of the radish leaves and root, and with carrot. The other juices help to repair the tissues which have been damaged by the sinus infection.

Of course it is also vital to adopt a natural healthy diet, cutting out all the refined carbohydrate foods which cause the build-up of mucus. It is also a good idea to switch from cow's milk, which is heavy and mucus-forming, to soya or goat's milk. When the horseradish has done its job, the heady, sweaty feeling will wane, as will the mucus. This is also a good treatment for coughs and catarrh.

Horseradish contains a good deal of vitamin C, far more than is found in many other vegetables, and also very large amounts of potassium and sulphur, manganese and calcium. It will improve the blood and the circulation, as it stimulates the capillaries of the blood as well as being good for water retention.

Lettuce Juice

This greatly underrated plant yields many surprises — it is an excellent treatment for a nervous cough, for diabetes, asthma, and good for calming the nervous system and digestive organs. It is believed to restore fertility — and even to calm down sexual ardour. Lettuce juice is said to help hair growth if it is mixed with spinach juice and drunk in quite large quantities of about a pint a day. It is so rich in minerals — iodine, phosphorus, iron, copper, calcium, cobalt, zinc, manganese and potassium — that it can help restore the natural mineral balance in the body. It also contains pro-vitamin A, and vitamins B, C and E.

Lettuce is an excellent source for anyone needing juice therapy because it contains so many alkaloids — including asparine, lactucine, lactucic acid and hyoscyamine. It has a slight laxative effect, with the side effect that ill-smelling stools are improved. As lettuce is such a good mineral and vitamin supply, do juice the entire plant because the outer leaves contain up to fifty times the amounts of these nutrients as the paler inner ones, although these are often more attractive.

Nettle Juice

The humble nettle has made a come-back in popular usage in recent years, particularly in shampoos and as a herbal tonic. But, in fact, it has for centuries been known as a most valuable herb and vegetable, and young nettles can be used in place of spinach. The nettle has many active constituents, including histamine, formic acid, gallic acid and hydroxytryptamine. There is a large amount of iron in the nettle plant and for this reason it is excellent for treating anaemia. It can help remove toxins from the blood, control diarrhoea and it is a diuretic which helps uric acid to be removed from the body. Herbalists recommend nettles to decrease mouth bleeding, for nervous eczema and to reduce the blood sugar level. The juice will help rheumatism sufferers and it will also help to relieve painful haemorrhoids.

The relative of the stinging nettle is the white dead-nettle; this actually comes from a completely different botanical family but it is also useful as a treatment for diarrhoea and as an astringent.

Onion Juice

Although there are many properties in the onion which are found in its relative, garlic, there are major differences between the two plants. Since the times of the ancient Greeks and the Romans the onion has been found to be excellent for the digestion and to purify the blood. Four hundred years ago the English herbalist, Nicholas Culpeper, wrote that vinegar and onion juice will remove skin blemishes; he also recommended it for removing worms in children, a remedy that was copied by German doctors two centuries later.

Onion juice is most useful as a remedy for catarrh and for any ailment affecting the respiratory tract, for colds and coughs, sore throats and bronchitis. When giving onion juice to children, mix it with warm water and a little honey to make it easier to take.

Onions contain a moderate amount of minerals and vitamins and a fairly high proportion of sugars. Its essential oils have a beneficial effect on the nervous system and clean any harmful bacteria out of the body, while at the same time having a stimulating effect on the bacteria which we need to be active inside the body.

Parsley Juice

It may surprise most people to learn that there is more vitamin C in the parsley plant than in any other commonly-used vegetable. It contains three times as much of the vitamin as oranges and more than blackcurrants. Parsley is also one of the best sources of pro-vitamin A — having about the same amount as carrots. It is high in iron and manganese and it contains apiol, a substance which is part of the female sex hormone oestrogen. Hence parsley is used in herbal medicine for regulating menstrual periods and increasing menstruation when needed.

It is a great pity to see parsley merely used as a decorative garnish. It is valuable for treating kidney stones, rheumatism, as a general stimulant and as a diuretic for treating water retention. It has been used to treat malaria and for everyday use it settles the stomach and stimulates the appetite.

Parsley juice is usually mixed with other juices and drunk in two-ounce doses three times a day. It is best to use fresh, rather than dried parsley, but frozen parsley is quite satisfactory and is the best way to store the leaves.

Potato Juice

One of the best pieces of news for the nutritionist in recent years has been the return to popularity of jacket potatoes, many restaurants serving them with a variety of fillings to make them really interesting. There is no doubt that the potato, complete with its jacket, is one of our most valuable vegetables — and in the winter it is one of the best sources of vitamin C, as well as being rich in potassium and many B vitamins. The potato is not fattening as it contains only about twenty per cent carbohydrate; it is only when fried that it becomes a fattening food.

Potatoes can be grated raw but some people find this too starchy. The green parts found on some potatoes must be removed as this is poisonous. Too much light on the plant during the growing period, or during storage after lifting, causes green potatoes to form.

Potato juice can cure eczema — but every case of eczema varies with the patient concerned and, as it is an allergy-based complaint, you should see a doctor and gain individual advice. The juice is good for the gastric tract and is used to treat gastric and duodenal ulcers; for gastritis, for haemorrhoids and constipation. Potato juice is best mixed with carrot or lemon juice to make it more palatable.

Radish Juice

Although radish juice is very valuable it should never be taken alone as it can be rather powerful. However, combined with carrot juice it helps to tone up the mucous membranes which get clogged up with catarrh. It can also be taken in a regime with horseradish juice. Radish juice soothes and heals the membranes and cleans out the mucus from the body, which the horseradish juice has already dissolved. It then restores the membranes to their natural state.

The juice is extracted from both the leaves and the roots of the radish plant, and it is a good source of potassium. The iron and magnesium contents are also high and it is by means of these minerals that the mucous membranes are soothed. It is also a good idea to cut down on mucus-forming foods, such as cow's milk, too much starchy white bread and cereals.

Spinach Juice

Everyone has heard of the wonderful properties of spinach — and it is true that even if it is not a miracle worker spinach is a really excellent source of nutrients. It is rich in vitamins, contains nearly as much pro-vitamin A, or carotene, as young carrots, as well as thiamine, riboflavin, nicotinic acid and folic acid — there is more of this last constituent in spinach than in any other vegetable except asparagus. There is as much vitamin C in spinach as there is to be found in oranges. It is an important source of iron and manganese, as well as calcium, sodium, phosphates, sulphates, chlorides — and a rather more rare mineral, cobalt. Cobalt has the ability to regenerate the blood — and, in fact, spinach juice is considered the finest juice anyone can take for nourishing the blood.

Raw juice does not have the effect of building up deposits of oxalic acid in kidney stones, which cooked spinach can do if eaten in very large quantities. Spinach juice is an excellent laxative and is an effective treatment for constipation, especially where cereal fibre has not worked. It will speed up recovery from illness for all convalescents and children and also rheumatism can be relieved by taking spinach juice.

For expectant and nursing mothers, it is an important source of important nutrients and will improve the quality of the milk for the baby.

Do juice spinach very soon after picking or many of its nutrients will be lost. Unlike many juices, it is possible to deep-freeze spinach juice, however, and store it in that way, or to pasteurize the juice and bottle it.

Tomato Juice

There is no comparison between canned juice and freshly-pressed tomato juice for natural goodness. It is mild but full of nutrition, with an abundance of minerals and vitamins. It is an ideal juice for children to take, especially if it is mixed with carrot and spinach juices. This makes a 'cocktail' which has a flavour which will appeal to most children and will give them a fine range of vitamins and minerals to help their blood and their general health. Tomato juice is good for anybody who has had a digestive upset, as it contains a high level of manganese. There are plenty of B vitamins in tomatoes, along with carotene (pro-vitamin A), and vitamins C, D, E and P. Iron, calcium, phosphorus and the trace elements copper and cobalt end the list which shows tomatoes to be an essential food.

Cooked tomatoes have less nutritional value than the raw juice, as do tomatoes which have been picked green and left to ripen afterwards. It is best to use freshly picked ripe tomatoes — they contain about twice the vitamin C content of the sort that were picked when still green.

Turnip Juice

This would be a good juice to take at the end of the winter, when the body can feel run-down and probably has little resistance to germs. It is a great tonic and is also good for the kidneys, especially if there are any stones present.

Turnip juice is slightly expectorant and so is good to use for chesty coughs and for bronchitis. It is best to use the whole turnip, complete with tops, as it is this part which gives the most nutritious goodness as a juice. Turnips are rich in calcium, good for the teeth and bones, and contain a great amount of vitamin C, especially when the tops are used raw. The type of calcium found in turnip tops does not contain too much oxalic acid so they are ideal for young children as this acid combines with calcium to prevent the mineral from being used by the body.

Watercress Juice
Watercress is one of the best sources of iodine which is essential for the thyroid gland to function properly. It is, anyway, a great tonic for the whole system and a good way of cleaning the blood. Watercress is also one of the best sources of sulphur and contains a whole list of minerals and vitamins, including sodium, calcium, potassium, iron and chlorides, vitamin C and carotene. It is too strong to take on its own, but diluted with clear spring water it makes a wonderful tonic. A good amount of folic acid, pantothenic acid, thiamine and nicotinic acid is to be found in watercress. The ancient Greek doctors knew of its powers to revitalize the body and for centuries it has been used to help the gall-bladder, liver, and the digestive system. Nowadays one of its principal uses in juice therapy is as a blood purifier and strengthener, and to expel the toxins that are believed to be the cause of arthritis and rheumatism. Watercress stimulates the circulation, regulates the intestines and, as it is a blood purifier, it will help any skin complaint, because poor quality blood results in poor quality skin.

Mix watercress juice with carrot, parsley and potato juice

to clear the lungs and to relieve emphysema. For rheumatism take watercress juice mixed with cucumber and beetroot juice. Anaemia can be helped by taking watercress and turnip top juice. Piles (haemorrhoids) can be reduced by taking watercress juice together with turnip roots; but it is essential to cut out all refined foods and to eat a balanced wholefood diet, along with the juice, for several months as the remedy will not work overnight.

3

A Raw Juice Diet

When a regime of juice therapy is started, it is best to fast for at least a day or two and then to start taking whatever juices are necessary to regain good health. After that the diet should be balanced and rely heavily on raw chopped salads, wholefoods, pulses and lentils. There is not much sense in drinking healthy fruit and vegetable juices and eating the wrong sorts of food. Even if only small drinks of fruit juices are taken, for a change and for their pleasant taste, they will not do any good if they are not incorporated into a balanced diet.

Good eating simply means eating the right foods in the right amounts. It means cutting out all over-refined foods made with white sugar and white flour. Cakes, bread, pastries and biscuits made with these foods should be avoided and that also includes sugary, starchy breakfast cereals, convenience foods and any food which contains artificial colours and flavourings. Instead, move towards wholefoods, the sorts of natural foods which have had nothing added to them or taken away from them: wholemeal flour, bread, whole grain cereals, brown rice, porridge oats, wholemeal pasta. People find that once they have switched away from other foods to wholefoods they actually enjoy the taste much more. Wholemeal bread is delicious and so unlike the soggy 'cotton wool texture' of white bread that it gives much more satisfaction, while at the same time providing the fibre that white bread cannot give. It is the same with wholemeal pastry which has a nutty taste and a dark colour. If, on occasions, a lighter-coloured pastry is needed, the bran can be sifted out and put into soups and stews.

It is also necessary to cut down on fats, salt and sugar of all kinds. All these foods have been linked with disease in recent years. Too much fat — of any kind, but especially of the hard, saturated animal fats such as butter and lard — causes a build-up of cholesterol in the blood-stream and can lead to arteriosclerosis, or heart disease. Too much salt can result in high blood-pressure. Try to do without it and use other flavourings, such as herbs and freshly ground black pepper, instead. Again, once the switch has been made, the taste-buds alter and will not notice the difference if other flavourings are used. Too much sugar rots the teeth and causes obesity which in turn can lead to many illnesses, including heart disease and diabetes. A sweet tooth should be discouraged in both adults and children. If necessary, food can be sweetened with fruit, especially dried fruit which is naturally sweet. Otherwise use a little honey, molasses or natural raw sugar — but all of these should be used sparingly, as they can help to put weight on as much as white sugar.

We need to have sufficient protein, carbohydrates, fats, vitamins and minerals to keep our bodies fit and functioning well. Once the right balance is achieved, the difference in energy levels will be noticeable.

Proteins

Proteins are compounds of carbon, hydrogen, oxygen and nitrogen. They are made up out of about twenty amino acids, some of which the body can manufacture for itself, and some which it cannot. There are eight of these that have to be obtained from food, and in the case of babies nine. The essential amino acids are isoleucine, leucine, lysine, methionine, phenylalanine, threonine, tryptophan and valine, with histidine for babies. All the body's cells are made up with protein, and the body needs a constant supply of the essential amino acids to keep the body tissues healthy. Different patterns of amino acids are necessary for the various structures of the body — the hair, skin and nails for instance.

Everyone needs protein in varying amounts — children and teenagers need it most. When body growth has finished, the adult needs protein to replace body tissue and to make digestive and other enzymes. Protein deficiency is a rarity in the Western world. It occurs mainly in the developing countries, and fatal diseases often result. People in the West tend to eat too much protein, thinking they have to pile it on their plates — and especially that of the bread-winner. In fact, children and adolescents need more than even the hardest-working manual labourer. Working adults need energy-giving foods which can be provided by carbohydrates and fats. A new-born baby needs five times as much protein as an adult, in proportion of weight pound for pound. As a child grows, the growth rate slows down and less protein is necessary.

As a rough guide, an adult needs about 45g of protein each day. Most of us eat far above that amount, but intake varies and some people can manage on less than the minimum while others are none the worse for eating several times as much. When it is realized that an ounce of cheese gives 25g of protein, it is easy to see that very small amounts of protein are needed each day. For babies and children under twelve months old, protein needs vary from between 15 and 20g a day, to between 30 and 53g a day at the age of seven or eight. Teenage girls need between 44 and 58g a day, while teenage boys need the very high amount of 50 to 75g every day.

There is no need to stick to animal protein only — that is, meat, fish, dairy products and eggs. Vegetable protein is excellent as it provides fibre and none of the hard fats of the animal proteins. Some vegetable proteins are used as meat substitutes — the soya bean, for instance. If more vegetable proteins were eaten, not only would a person's general diet and health improve but their bank balance too. The vegetable proteins include pulses — all the dried beans and lentils — and grains, brown rice, oats and millet, potatoes and nuts. Nuts are higher in fat than grains and pulses so it is best not to eat too many. Texturized vegetable protein, or tvp, is manufactured usually from soya beans, to look and taste like meat and it is a useful variation to other vegetable proteins. It is also good to have a packet in the store cupboard ready for emergencies.

Fats

We need fats for energy but we do not need as much as most people tend to eat; what is not burnt up as energy is laid down as body fat, which will lead to obesity and illness. In the last few years much has been said about the need to eat the polyunsaturated, softer fats made from vegetable oils rather than the harder, saturated animal fats. This is true, because the harder fats are high in cholesterol which is laid down in deposits in the arteries and can lead to heart disease, but we are still eating too much fat of all kinds.

When research on this subject was first carried out, it was noticed that people living in the poorer Third World countries did not have much heart disease in comparison with the Western world. However, when people from these countries came to live in the West and changed their diet, they too became susceptible to heart disease. The rate of heart disease in Britain remains one of the highest in the world, whereas in countries like America, where people have become more aware of the need to change their diet, the rates have fallen. There are other factors involved in heart disease, and doctors know that smoking and stress play their part, but high levels of cholesterol have been found in the arteries of patients with heart disease. One of the most famous studies on heart disease was started in 1949 in a town in Massachusetts, USA. Research scientists monitored the health of five thousand men for a number of years, and came to the conclusion that men on a high-fat diet were more at risk of contracting the disease. In the under-developed countries where the average saturated fat intake is just over 30g a day, heart disease is rare but in the West, where people eat as much as 110g a day, heart disease is commonplace.

Therefore it is best to cut down on all hard animal fats and use instead a little of the polyunsaturated fats made from vegetable oils. Do beware, though, as some plant fats, such as coconut oil and palm oil, are highly saturated. Some naturally unsaturated fats can be artificially saturated by forcing in extra hydrogen during food processing and then the fat ends up with a totally different structure. Polyunsaturated fats also contain just as many calories as the hard saturated fats which is another reason for cutting down all round on fats. Choose vegetable oils and cook with corn, sunflower or safflower oils instead of lard or butter. If meat is eaten, cut away the fatty parts, choose leaner cuts and eat less lamb and pork, more chicken and fish.

Try not to fry food — grill, poach or boil instead. Eat only between three and six eggs a week as they are rich in cholesterol. Instead of adding butter or margarine to vegetables, add a sprinkling of freshly chopped herbs. Rather than roasting potatoes in a lot of fat, bake them in their jackets and do not coat them with butter but use a low calorie filling such as cottage cheese, mushrooms or onions. Try to switch to skimmed, soya or goat's milk as full-fat cow's milk is rich in cholesterol. Eat less high-fat cheese — go for low or medium-fat cheeses such as cottage cheese, ricotta, Edam or Camembert. Cheddar and Brie are rich in saturated fats. It is a good idea to cut down on pastries and cakes generally. Fruit can be eaten for dessert. Natural yogurt flavoured with fruit is delicious, or it can be used as a topping instead of cream or ice-cream on desserts.

These are some helpful ideas on how to cut down fat intake. When people start to think about the 'hidden extras' contained in their diet they begin to realize just how much fat they do eat each day.

Carbohydrates

Dieters always think they have to cut out the carbohydrates from their food first, when in fact the extra calories come mainly from energy-rich fats. Slimmers have always tended to shy away from bread and potatoes but it is the fat that is added to these foods that make them laden with calories. It is the butter or even the margarine on the bread, and the heavy cheese topping, that lays down the fat on the body. It is not the potato that makes us fat, but the fat that it is fried in to make into chips.

Plants make carbohydrates out of water and carbon dioxide, using the sun's energy. The plant's rigid structure is composed of cellulose, which is one form of carbohydrate, but this is passed through the body as fibre. The two main types of carbohydrate, that can be digested, are starch and sugar.

In poorer countries cereals such as rice, oats and barley, play a large part in the diet. In our affluent society we have neglected these foods largely in favour of bread, flour-based foods and potatoes for our main sources of starch. Grains such as rice contain high-quality protein as well as carbohydrate. Natural starches, bread containing wholemeal flour using all the wheat, unrefined brown rice, and other whole grains, fill the body up and it stays feeling full as the food takes longer to pass through. Hence it is possible to slim while on a diet containing this sort of carbohydrate — as the successful high-fibre diet books have shown in recent years. Try to insist on wholemeal flour made from stoneground wholewheat, and the same goes for bread, as this is of the highest quality. Some breads are merely coloured to look brown and are not wholemeal at all.

By switching to these carbohydrates there will be less chance of contracting other Western diseases caused by constipation — diverticulitis, varicose veins, appendicitis, colitis and even cancer of the colon.

Sugar

We do not need sugar for health. From the way that so many British householders keep stocks of sugar in their store cupboards, it would seem that sugar is a necessity for life. It gives calories but these are empty calories, providing no nutrients at all. The body can convert starch in the same way as sugar, and starch, if unrefined, does give many nutrients for energy. Yet while we eat less starch, sugar consumption has risen dramatically in the past century. The end result has been dental decay, obesity and illness. Until recently people regarded false teeth and a middle-aged paunch as a fact of life. Now we know that this need not be so if we eat sensibly and eat natural foods. All sugar is harmful if taken in excess, whether it is white, brown, granulated or powdered, syrup or even honey. Raw sugar and honey do contain some trace elements, and less is needed especially of molasses to give the same amount of sweetness; but all sugar should be taken sparingly.

Sugar has a simpler structure than starch so it takes less time for it to be absorbed. This gives a person a 'lift' very soon afterwards, which people used to think was a good thing. Now we know that after a short time, when the sugar has been absorbed, there is a downward swing once more. Without taking any extra sugar, the blood generally keeps its own level of sugar naturally. If energy is needed it would be better to eat a sandwich made from wholemeal bread, or a full meal containing bread or other starch, which will then give a feeling of fullness for a long while as it takes more time to be absorbed by the stomach.

Once again, it must be stressed that sugary soft drinks do no good to the teeth or the rest of the body. Fresh vegetable and fruit drinks have their own natural sweetness, leave a clean taste in the mouth and clean the system generally. Raw juices leave one feeling much better than does a sugary glass of squash or even a supposedly healthy drink like commercial blackcurrant juice, which is full of sugar and artificial additives.

Minerals

We know a fair amount about vitamins and why they are needed, but most people know very little about minerals. They know that iron is necessary for the blood to be strong and to prevent anaemia and calcium is required for strong teeth and bones. That is usually about all we do know. In the past few years there has grown up a great deal of interest in minerals, and rightly so, for they also contain the key to good health. From reading the chapter on the properties of individual fruits and vegetables, it will be seen how many of them are high in minerals and what each particular type will do for the body. Over twenty different minerals are now recognized as being vital for health. Soon a few more may be added to the list, some of which are metals. Much research is now going on to discover more about this fascinating aspect of our diet.

Minerals serve three main functions in keeping the body healthy. They are the basic material for the bones and teeth, especially calcium, phosphorus, and magnesium. They act as controllers of the balance, amount and composition of the body liquids, both inside and outside the body cells; sodium and chlorine act outside the cells, while potassium, magnesium and phosphorus work inside the cells. The main job for most minerals is to act as triggers for the enzyme processes in the body. These enzyme processes are vital to every cell. Some minerals are present in only tiny amounts, so tiny in fact that they are called the trace elements because there is only a trace of them in the body. This was probably the reason for the neglect of minerals as a study. It was thought that as they were present in such small amounts they could not be considered important. In fact our bodies contain a far larger amount of minerals than they do of vitamins. With the improvement in scientific research so have the methods of identifying and measuring minerals and assessing their importance also improved. But there is still a long way to go.

There are many times when vital minerals may be missing

from the food we eat. At other times they may be lost before our bodies can use them. If they are not present in the right balance, then our health suffers. It is important to remember that while we need the balance of minerals in small amounts they can be dangerous in large quantities. Some minerals are even positively dangerous to take at all — the heavy metals, cadmium, lead and mercury. These are poisons and while we can survive with a little inside us, as a result of pollution in the atmosphere from lead fumes in petrol, for example, there is no saying what damage is being done to people's health in the long term. One of the minerals which we take to excess is sodium — salt. After reading about the various fruits and vegetables it can be realized how much food contains sodium. We get enough salt in our food without having to add it in either cooking or at the table; instead, it is better to flavour with fresh herbs and freshly ground black pepper. It is also a good idea to eat less of the salty foods — bacon and canned meats, sausages and cheese such as Cheddar. In that way, problems of high blood-pressure, and the danger of heart attacks, will be reduced.

Calcium can be taken to excess in both babies and adults. This is usually caused by taking too much vitamin D, or being over-sensitive to it. Although the effects can be serious, leading to permanent damage or even fatalities in babies, the condition is rare and most people do not store too much calcium beyond their needs. Minerals such as iodine and cobalt, which would cause great harm if taken in excess, are not sold for general supplements. Copper can be taken in over-doses and it is believed that it is responsible for heart attacks. A high intake of copper affects the way in which zinc works in the body — but there are ways in which copper intake can be reduced. Copper water piping can result in far higher than normal levels of the mineral in the water supply, especially in areas were the water is already acidic. Do not drink water from the hot tap which has copper piping, or use it in the kettle or for cooking.

Fluoride can be poisonous if too much is taken, and, where there is a high level of it in the water supply, people's teeth become mottled in colour. There are a few doctors who think that fluoride in the water supply is responsible for deaths from cancer, mainly in the USA. The move to fluoridate water supplies has been halted in many countries while there is any doubt about the safety of the mineral. Dentists have welcomed fluoride as an aid to keeping teeth free from bacteria but it is commonly recognized nowadays that it is sugary foods which cause tooth decay and it is more necessary to stop eating so many of the wrong foods. There is also a filter available on the market which can be attached to a household tap and it will remove flouride from your water supply. This is not a distiller, which leaves water without any of the minerals which are good to take and which makes water unpleasant to drink.

Where mineral deficiency is concerned, for most of us it is usually quite late by the time it is diagnosed and already much damage may have been done. Small deficiencies can go on for years before they are finally discovered. Looking at the deficiency in any mineral as a cause of illness is still a new idea and it is still regarded with some scepticism, as such a tiny amount is needed by the body at one time. Yet it is recognized that iodine and B_{12} deficiencies are serious, and they are also needed in tiny quantities. Many studies are going on, particularly on the importance of enough zinc and selenium in our diet. It is found, especially in the case of selenium, that where the soil is depleted of the mineral that mineral is not present in food, and this can result in various illnesses. On the other hand, in selenium-rich soils such as are found in the Andes, in the Hunza region of north Pakistan, and nearer home, in the Cork region of Ireland and around Sheringham in Norfolk, the people tend to live longer, healthier lives. They grow their own fruit and vegetables and benefit from the selenium that comes with the crops.

Vitamins

Vitamins have been described as organic substances necessary for life. They are vital for our growth, health and well-being. Our bodies cannot function without them and, with a few exceptions, they cannot be made by our bodies or synthesized by the body. Vitamins are found in minute amounts in all organic food. Vitamin pills are necessary at times for certain conditions where extra nutrition is needed (and that covers many different situations in twentieth-century living), but they are not food replacements.

First, and foremost, vitamins should be obtained from a good balanced diet. Fruit and vegetable juices can help to provide all the daily vitamin requirements of any child or adult. Some vitamins are water-soluble and the body cannot store them, so they must be replaced every day; these are the B complex vitamins and vitamins C and P. The fat-soluble vitamins — A, D, E, K, are stored for long periods in the body. There are thirteen known vitamins at present. The B-complex group is rather confusing as there are gaps in the numbering; the numbers in between do not exist, as yet. Research is still going on and in a few years we may know more about vitamins, like minerals, and more may be identified.

There is a danger of storing too much A and D in the body but these vitamins have to be taken in huge amounts for this to happen, so nobody should be unduly alarmed about this aspect of diet. Vitamin A is found in fish-liver oil, liver, dairy produce and eggs, and sometimes it is added to margarine. Carotene, which is converted into vitamin A, is found in carrots, spinach and yellow and dark green vegetables. Fatty fish, eggs and sunlight are the main sources of vitamin D. Vitamin E is found in many foods, especially wheatgerm, sunflower oil and eggs, wholemeal cereals, broccoli and human milk. The main sources of vitamin K are leafy vegetables and cereals. Many foods make up the vitamin B complex from animal and dairy produce (B_{12}) to wholegrain cereals, peanuts and bananas (B_6). Citrus fruits, blackcurrants, green leafy vegetables, green peppers and liver are the principal sources of vitamin C. New potatoes are high in vitamin C, but much of the vitamin is lost with long storage and over-cooking.

Oranges and lemons contain the largest concentrations of bioflavonoids — but there is a whole list of fruits and vegetables which, when juiced, provide these rich substances. Bio means active; flavonoids refer to the crystalline substance which makes some foods yellow coloured — foods such as oranges and lemons, watermelons and the other varieties of citrus fruits. There are other less obvious foods containing bioflavonoids, such as cabbage, peppers, tomatoes and strawberries. The main constituents of bioflavonoids are the vitamin C, K and P, as well as ascorbic acid and hesperidin. Hesperidin is a crystalline substance which is contained more in the peel and the pulp of the fruit — so the pith and pulp should be added in the juicer and not discarded. The peel should be sucked or chewed if possible. Bioflavonoids also contain other vitamins, minerals, amino acids and protopectin.

Oranges were first given to ward off scurvy; this was an affliction which made life especially hard for the sailors away for months at a time and with very little nourishment to hand. Nowadays it is also recognized that citrus fruits have another role to play, improving the strength and permeability of the capillary walls in the body. Vitamin C is not stored by the body, so it is extremely easy for deficiencies to arise. People suffering with rheumatoid arthritis have very fragile capillaries and so they would benefit from taking bioflavonoids in the form of raw juice therapy. Other diseases which have been successfully treated with bioflavonoids include rheumatic fever, haemorrhages, diabetic retinopathy, and arteriosclerosis. In the case of the last condition, blood vessels lose some of their permeability so that nutrients are lost to the body; this can be helped if bioflavonoids and calcium are given. Citrus fruit juices are extremely valuable for pregnant women, whose capillary walls need to be strengthened to cope with the increased fluid retention and oedema. A daily dose of eight ounces of citrus fruit juices is recommended. It is well known that taking vitamin C in large doses helps a cold to go through its course more quickly and there is no more pleasant and refreshing treatment than to drink citrus fruit and other juices containing bioflavonoids.

Fibre

Years ago the term used for this sort of food was 'roughage' and it was thought to be merely waste matter. This was because fibre passes through the body mostly unchanged, as the alimentary canal in the human body does not have the enzymes to break this food down. So little was known about fibre that about forty years ago patients with bowel complaints were put on to sloppy baby-type foods rather than make their poor digestive systems work too hard. More recently fibre has become fashionable in nutrition terms and the high-fibre diet has been successful for many people. Fibre can help take off weight because it acts like a sponge, mopping up waste and liquids as it passes through the body. It speeds up the transit time of waste materials through the body, it dilutes toxins and increases the bulk of the motions passed.

People who eat more fibre feel fuller for longer periods of time, so they need less to eat. Constipation leads to lethargy and obesity but a person eating a lot of fibre will not become constipated in the first place. They will also have a greater feeling of well-being and more energy to take exercise. In this way they will become fitter. The medical profession is urging people to eat more fibre. A good average is about 30g a day. Most people in the Western world eat a good deal less than this — around 20g or less a day — whereas in the underdeveloped countries people are eating more than 60g of fibre every day. It has been found that Africans and Asians do not suffer from the diseases caused by constipation — diverticular disease, colitis, appendicitis, and cancer of the colon. This has been linked to their high-fibre diet.

What is fibre? It consists of a large group of substances that make up the supporting structure in plant cell walls, and parts of plants close to them, such as the white pith of fruit. Fibre is a term that also covers plant gums, and pectin. Foods that are high in fibre are unrefined brown rice, fruit, especially dried fruit, nuts, vegetables (especially the outer leaves) including dried pulses and lentils, wholegrain cereals, wholemeal bread, crispbread and pasta.

Food Processing

This has been going on in one form or another for centuries. People used salt to cure meat to give it a longer life and they coated meat in brine for the same reason. Smoked fish is another example of traditional food processing. Modern technology has brought in a whole range of food processing methods which have given us a greater choice of foods which need less time to cook at home, and foods can be kept palatable for longer periods than in the past. When so many of us live a long way from the source of many foods, it is important that food can be kept fresh while in transit and while it sits on the supermarket shelf.

All plants and animals start to deteriorate a short time after harvesting or death; so some processing, of necessity, must be used. It varies from canning and bottling, to various types of drying, and to freezing. The arguments against eating a lot of processed food are obvious in that processed food tends to be high in fat, salt, and sugar. It is also hard to tell how nutritious processed food actually is, because so many technological changes have taken place with it. Some foods are safer to consume — pasteurized milk, for instance, and although processing involves some loss of nutrients, this may be no more than happens to natural, fresh food which is left uneaten for several days. On the whole, however, it is better to avoid many of the modern convenience foods as much as possible and stay with the natural foods, eating them while they are still fresh. Natural, freshly-pressed juices are one of the best ways to supplement diet, and the very best substitute for modern cold drinks. Even the fruit juice cartons found in supermarkets have been processed in some form and, in some cases, watered down.

Food Additives

Linked to food processing are the additives used to preserve food, especially necessary in the industrialized countries where populations live a long way from food sources. A whole industry has grown up around this need, continuing a tradition that has come down to us through the centuries — ever since salt and spices were added to foods to disguise

deterioration or to give more flavour. Nowadays there are
about three thousand food additives — although two thousand
at least are flavourings, and many of these are herbs and spices.
The remaining additives on the list, however, have given rise
to anxiety. There are preservatives, colourings, antioxidants
(these stop food going rancid) and other types of additives.
Some are functional, others are purely cosmetic — making
the product look more acceptable to the customer.

Many people think there is no justification in using
cosmetic additives at all. A powerful lobby has grown up
in recent years, and several food colours previously considered
safe have been withdrawn in several countries because of
doubts about their safety. One example of this is baby foods:
in Britain, the baby food manufacturers no longer colour
the food that goes into jars and tins for babies and toddlers.

For centuries nitrates and nitrites have been used to cure
meats like bacon, ham and tongue. These chemicals prevent
bacteria forming on the meat and give it its pink tinge and
flavour. Nowadays a controversy has arisen because it has
been found that nitrates and nitrites can be converted into
small amounts of nitrosamines in the body. This can cause
stomach cancer. The amount of risk for anyone who eats
these meats is not known, and of course not everyone who
eats bacon, ham or tongue will contract cancer. The incidence
of the disease is actually on the wane, and the meat must
be protected from germs. On the other hand, if this is a risk,
should we cut down on these foods as a safeguard? Similar
arguments surround the use of antioxidants such as BHT
and BHA, and sulphur dioxide — which is put into all sorts
of drinks from wine and beer to soft drinks, as well as foods.

In the USA many food labels contain nutritional
information, but often it is so technical that it only serves
to confuse the customer. Other countries, especially the EEC

group, give additive code names and these can be checked
out. In Britain manufacturers need only give the function
of an additive and not its name. Some products, such
as biscuits, do not have to carry any information at all.

The answer, surely, is to cut down on buying these foods
to a minimum and buy as much natural food as possible.
Cut out soft drinks which have so many additives and switch
to freshly-pressed fruit and vegetable juices made in the juicer
at home.

Slimming Diets

Crash diets, which make people lose weight fast, are not good
for the body — nor do they have a lasting effect. Slow, steady
loss of weight is healthy and the weight is more likely to
be shed forever — if a regime of eating lots of raw fruit and
vegetable is followed. This type of diet provides vitamins
and minerals that are rapidly absorbed into the system. Many
diets, especially those which concentrate on protein, are
damaging because they take so many minerals out of the
body. The feeling of lethargy and constant craving for food
is absent as raw fruits and vegetables provide all the nutrients
needed for health and vitality, plus plenty of fibre which
is extremely filling. On a raw food and juice diet there is
no need to feel hungry. Juices and raw fruit and vegetables
will also make a slimmer feel clear-headed and well — a
change from the depressive feeling many other diets give
to people.

Carrot, spinach, beetroot and cucumber are all juices
especially good for a slimmer to take. Take fairly large
quantities of fresh carrot juice and mix it with smaller
amounts of the other three vegetables. Carrot juice is so good
for slimmers because it has an abundance of vitamins and
minerals and is the best way to get rid of poisons from the
body. It leaves the muscles toned-up and the mind more vital.

Exercise does not take off the fat as much as simply eating less of the foods that are fattening and more of the foods which give most nutrients to the body. On the other hand, exercise tones the body and adds to the feeling of well-being. Slimmer people feel more active, so as the diet progresses it should be easier to exercise — indeed, exercise and a good diet, packed with raw fruits and vegetables and their juices, is a recipe for a slim and happy life.

4

Raw Juice Therapy

Before any treatment with raw vegetable or fruit juices can be started the toxins that have caused the condition in question, whether it is rheumatism or a skin complaint, an internal disease or a childhood ailment, must be removed. All the waste matter that has built up in the body is loosened and then moved on. It is absorbed once more by the bloodstream and, in due course, is passed through the body. Sometimes during this process the symptoms can worsen but it really is probably a case of 'getting worse before it gets better'. For young active people this rather difficult time is more apparent and shows itself usually in the first six weeks of treatment. In older and weaker people with a chronic illness the toxins are removed more slowly and so no worsening of the symptoms may be seen at all.

Raw juice therapy fits in with all nature cures as pioneered by the doctors of the last century — Dr J. H. Kellogg, Dr Henry Lindlahr and Father Sebastian Kniepp among others. These men used the simplest of methods to get their results. They saw disease as the outcome of a poor state of mind and body where germs could flourish. They used healing plants alongside fresh air and sunlight, natural clear water and rich earth to grow the plants, for their healing regimes. Their views are even more relevant today as so many people poison their bodies by eating refined foods with all the goodness taken away and with foods full of chemical flavourings and colourings. We need to return to natural food and turn our backs on synthetic foods. All this was seen as far back as a hundred years ago. Any nature treatment starts with the idea that the whole person and organism should be treated as a unity. This holistic outlook is, of course, at odds with orthodox doctors who merely treat the symptoms without going to the root cause.

Often the sort of patient who comes to a practitioner who uses juice therapy is a desperate person who has tried all other forms of medicine and treatments. Where the orthodox has failed, a natural cure will often work. The first thing to do is eliminate all over-refined foods from the diet. Then after a fast of about three days, in which time the body has a chance to pass out all the excess waste matter, raw juices can be given. Again, it must be stressed that self-diagnosis and treatment is not a good idea. Weakness and a worsening of the symptoms may be felt before there is a return to health. This should be closely followed and analysed by a practitioner who knows full well all the implications of the treatment. On the other hand, raw juice therapy does not conflict with other forms of treatment and often can be used in conjunction with them. The patient will be advised to take between one and eight pints of juice each day, but never to take more than feels comfortable. It is not always right to say that the more juice that is consumed the quicker the result will be, but there will not be much benefit from taking too little juice or for too short a time. So, less than a pint a day is likely to be ineffective, as would be a course of treatment that lasted for less than a month. While an experienced practitioner could get quick results with less juice than is recommended, that would be because of the individual's particular case.

There is absolutely no harm in taking a glass or two of fresh fruit or vegetable juice every day to keep in good health; but if therapy is needed to overcome a disease or even an ailment, then it is best to consult a qualified practitioner.

Arthritis

Arthritis is usually caused by an infection, or by a long forgotten injury, which has built up infection. In the majority of cases of arthritis there has also been a history of poor diet, with resulting vitamin and mineral deficiencies. Arthritis sufferers have been found to have lived on a diet high in heavy starches, sugars and fats, low in fresh fruits and vegetables. They also often show a lack of the vitamin B complex. Of course, any of the symptoms of arthritis — inflammation, pain and swelling in the joints, and often a fever — should not be treated by the individual. It needs a thorough examination by a qualified naturopath or doctor who will then treat the symptoms according to the individual's needs. As so often a dietary deficiency is apparent, if a doctor does not give dietary advice then it is up to the individual to examine their diet to see if they can do anything to improve it: nearly always they can.

Acute arthritis is believed to be caused by an infection in the blood-stream that is carried from other parts of the body; infected teeth, tonsils or sinuses may be the cause. Constipation and other ailments of the intestinal tract, which can lead to infection, are another cause of the disease. In the case of childhood arthritis, it is often thought that germs left over from some childhood illnesses may be the cause. Complete relaxation and warmth are essential in the treatment of acute arthritis. Heat helps to ease the pain as it makes the swelling and inflammation go down and keeps the circulation going. The fever has to be reduced and the infection must be treated with a complete treatment of the deficiencies found in the diet which gave the disease a stronghold in the first place.

Children and young adults seem to be more prone to rheumatic fever than older people. They must be kept extremely warm at all times and should not do much exercise for many months as the heart is often weakened by the illness. While the fever lasts, a more or less liquid diet of thinned-down food should be given which can have wheatgerm or brewer's yeast added to it to provide vitamin B. Thin soups can be given and lots of juices — both fruit and vegetable.

Liquids are ideal for an arthritis sufferer because they are so easy to digest, with a recommended daily intake of three or four quarts of juices and water, with smaller amounts of thin soups and other liquids. The toxins coming from the infection must be eliminated from the body. Good fruit juices to drink are apple, pineapple, grape, orange, pear and grapefruit; vegetable juices can include carrot, celery and cucumber. These juices will give the patient the vitamins and minerals needed to make the body more resistant to infection. They will also help the process of using other nutrients in the body to get to work and start the healing that is needed. Other foods, provided they are not sweet, fatty, or heavy in starch, can be gradually added to the diet as the patient gets a little better. There is no need to build up the protein side of the diet too soon. If gout is diagnosed, meat should be restricted. The ultimate aim is for a well-balanced diet, high in vitamins and minerals, which will provide enough nutrients to cut any infection down to a minimum and eventually eliminate it altogether if possible.

There are two types of chronic arthritis. One is rheumatoid arthritis and the other is osteoarthritis. The first is also called chronic infectious arthritis and the second is given the alternative name of chronic degenerative arthritis. The infectious type can usually be traced back to a history of a previous attack of acute arthritis. People of all ages can be affected but it does tend to attack the more youthful end of the population. The degenerative or osteoarthritis usually affects elder people, from middle age onwards; often there is also a hardening of the arteries. Overweight and constipated people are at risk, and so are women in the menopause stage. This type of arthritis is accompanied by a build-up of calcium, sodium urate, bone and cartilage at the joints. These become painful, swollen and enlarged. The areas affected are usually the fingers, wrists, knees and ankles — but any of the joints can be attacked in this way. Careful diagnosis by a doctor is absolutely essential because sometimes arthritis can extend to other areas such as the leg muscles, the shoulders, back or arms. There is also a danger then that confusion can arise and the sufferer may think that he or she has lumbago, sciatica or neuritis. It is essential to reduce acidity in the body. Constipation must be eliminated for good. Foods that are easily digested — and juices come into this category — are needed. This is a diet recommended for arthritis sufferers:

First thing:

Half a lemon, juiced and added to a glass of warm water. Always dilute lemon juice.

Breakfast:

Apple juice, orange juice
or
a baked apple
or
grapefruit, prunes, apricots or strawberries
and
soft-boiled or poached egg
with
wholemeal or rye toast with a little vegetable margarine
To drink: herb tea, sweetened with a little honey or with
goat's milk.

Mid-morning:

Apple juice (8 fl oz/230ml)

Lunch:

Start with an 8 fl oz (230ml) glass of juice, either carrot,
carrot and celery or carrot/beet/cucumber.
Follow with salads, with cottage cheese added, with olive
oil and lemon dressing. Substitute cottage cheese for fish
if liked.
One slice of wholemeal bread thinly spread with vegetable
margarine.
For a dessert, choose a banana, orange or other fruit. A jelly
made with fresh fruit juice and agar-agar would be beneficial,
as would a helping of natural yogurt, perhaps with some
fruit whipped in.
To drink: one cup of herb tea, mineral water.

Mid-afternoon:

Carrot juice (8 fl oz/230ml)

Dinner:

Vegetable juice — either carrot, carrot and celery, or carrot/beet/cucumber.

Follow with a hot dish of baked or grilled fish, or a small serving of lean meat or chicken, with a selection of lightly-steamed vegetables which could include carrots, spinach, celery, broccoli, and runner or French beans. Alternatively mix a salad using cooked vegetables, and add chopped fruit into the salad — apple and celery are a good combination. Pour a little lemon and oil dressing over the salad or make a dressing from natural yogurt. One slice of wholemeal or rye bread with a little vegetable margarine.

Dessert — fresh fruit, fresh fruit salad with yogurt topping, portion of low-fat or cottage cheese and wholemeal biscuits. To drink: mineral water, herb tea or goat's milk.

Late evening:

Either celery juice or carrot and celery juice (8 fl oz/230ml).

Of course this is a guide only, and lunch and dinner menus can be interchanged. It is important to drink enough water each day to make a minimum of eight glasses of liquids. If an attack of arthritis occurs, increase the fluid intake to between twelve and fourteen glasses of liquids a day. This can include herb teas, soups and milk as well as juices.

Bronchitis and Coughs

Any bronchial infections, catarrh and coughs need to be treated by cleansing the system. A fast for two or three days, taking only juices, has proved to be very effective. Take diluted fruit juices about every two hours. Unsweetened blackcurrant tea, which can be made from blackcurrant purée, or lemon juice sweetened with honey are good remedies, as are apple juice and grape juice. By leaving food alone the body has a chance to get rid of the toxins that cause these infections. Digestion of food is difficult at this time anyway, and it is better to purge the system before going back to any food.

Cancer

Raw fruit and vegetable juices are used all over the world in treating cancer. Juices have the advantage of rapidly giving the sick body the nutrients it needs to fight the disease while putting the least amount of strain on the digestive system. Cancer is now one of the biggest killers, especially in the Western world, where most of the five million deaths from cancer occur each year. Modern drugs have dangerous and unpleasant side-effects, such as hair loss, and still have not vastly improved the situation. Drugs and treatments such as laser therapy are used to kill off the cancerous growths, but they do not give the body a chance to do its own healing and to build up resistance against the illness.

Some of the anti-cancer therapies based on raw juices use great quantities of the required fruit and vegetables to achieve results. One of the pioneers of raw food diets was Max Gerson who tried various diets to cure himself of sickening headaches and migraine attacks, a complaint which ran in his family. Having cured himself by eating large amounts of fresh fruit and vegetables, he started to cure others suffering from the same complaint; through chance he started to cure people also affected by lupus, a rare form of tuberculosis of the skin. He realized that his way of eating gave the body the chance to heal itself. It was able to cure a whole range of ailments and he went on to treat all kinds of disease, including mental illness.

Gerson ultimately became famous for his work on cancer.

He came to the conclusion that a mineral imbalance is responsible for all illness, including cancer. In his patients he saw that there was usually too much sodium and too little potassium. This could be corrected by cutting out foods containing sodium and concentrating on potassium-rich raw foods. Potassium needs some sodium and works with it to regulate the body's water balance and normalize heart rhythms. Potassium works just inside the cells, while sodium works just outside them. Nerve and muscle functions suffer when there exists an imbalance of sodium and potassium. Potassium helps to send oxygen to the brain, helps to get rid of waste matter from the body, reduces blood-pressure and fights allergies. It is found in all leafy green vegetables, citrus fruits, watercress, bananas, and potatoes, as well as sunflower seeds and in mint. The enemies of potassium are alcohol, coffee, sugar and diuretics from the chemist. Raw foods which contain plenty of potassium are able to clean out the body and organize the white blood cells to fight and kill cancer cells.

Beetroot has been used to treat cancer patients in various clinics within the past forty-five years. As long ago as 1938 a doctor called Kunstmann used beetroot in leukaemia cases, with good results. In Hungary, in 1950, beetroot was again used on cancer patients, either mashed or given as raw juice diluted in water when it was found that the patient could manage better on juice than solid food. The success rate was fifteen out of sixteen cases, with the growths reduced, the patients gaining weight and their blood count improving. This led to continued success at the clinic, which was run by Dr S. Firenczi.

A couple of examples show how successful beetroot juice therapy can be. Two patients had similar tumours — one affecting the prostate, the other a woman with the female equivalent, cancer of the uterus. The prostate patient took daily doses of beetroot juice, and after a month did not need the catheter which had had to be used at the beginning of treatment at the clinic. The catheter was not used again. He had improved so much that he was mobile once more. The female patient could not take beetroot juice or the solid vegetable. By contrast with the prostate patient, she was unable to leave her bed, kept on losing weight and after three and a half months had lost even more weight, while the male patient had gained twenty one pounds. Another patient was admitted to the clinic with recurring breast cancer. She was put on beetroot juice therapy straight away and showed a decided improvement.

John B. Lust, writing more than twenty years ago on beetroot juice therapy, outlined a ten day programme to reduce cancerous growths. He suggested that the regime could be repeated every two months until the condition was cleared up. The length of treatment in total would depend on the size of the tumour and the general health of the individual. On the first and second day, he said, there should be a short fast to cleanse the system. Only a glass of diluted lemon juice should be drunk on getting up and then, during the rest of the day, only grapefruit and/or orange juice as wanted, but not less than 16 fl oz (460ml) each day. Absolute rest is essential — even baths are not recommended because they can be draining, and showers are suggested instead. On the fourth, fifth and sixth days, take lemon juice and water as before but take 8 fl oz (230ml) of citrus juice and 16 fl oz (460ml) of other juices. The best combinations are probably carrot and beetroot juice in equal quantities, or carrot juice (6 fl oz/175ml), beetroot juice (5 fl oz/140ml) and cucumber juice, again 5 fl oz (140ml). Meals should be made up with fresh raw fruits — apples, grapefruits, oranges, pears, pineapples and strawberries when they are in season.

Some exercises may be started at this stage, plus some hydrotherapy. The combination of fresh fruits and raw juices should, with some activity, be enough for normal bowel movements to start again, if as is quite possible, the patient has been constipated. On the seventh to tenth day the patient can start to eat meals of a light nature. Diluted lemon juice should still be taken first thing, and breakfast should consist of fruit and some fruit juice. A starch food such as wholemeal bread or a jacket potato with a raw salad can be eaten at lunchtime. This should start to provide the fibre necessary for normal bowel movements to resume. Cucumber and watercress can be included in the chopped raw salad and a glass of raw juice should be taken, with some fruit for dessert.

In the evening the main meal should consist of steamed beetroot and spinach, or any of the other vegetables outlined above, with a jacket potato. Add some cheese and a little milk, preferably goat's milk, and take some fresh fruit to round off the meal. Before going to bed take a glass of one of the recommended raw juice combinations. Every meal should include at least two of the vegetables recommended for tumour cases. Meals should be varied so that a well-balanced diet is being given and, if the patient is hungry between meals, some raw fruit or a glass of raw vegetable juice can be taken.

Colitis

Another name for colitis is 'irritable bowel syndrome'. Symptoms show themselves as distension, cramps, and constipation alternating with diarrhoea. A high-fibre diet, with fruit and vegetable juices, will ease the condition. The main causes of the illness are generally longstanding constipation or a nervous condition. Usually a high-fibre diet helps the situation, as we now know that bowel habits are generally better when people eat more fibre.

Simple colitis is an irritated colon. There is an uncomfortable feeling of flatulence, the abdomen feels distended, there is pain and diarrhoea, which comes after a period of being constipated. Underlying causes are nervous disorders and a poor diet lacking in nutrients and fibre. A high-fibre diet also protects against cancer of the colon. If laxatives, enemas and colonic irrigations are tried, especially without the advice of a qualified practitioner, more damage than good will be the result. Some people accept constipation as a fact of life, when that need never be the case if they have enough fibre in a well-balanced diet.

In the treatment of colitis, all irritating types of food should be avoided — such as heavily-spiced dishes, fried foods and highly processed and coloured foods, as all these may make the already-inflamed colon more irritated. Fruit and vegetable juices are the ideal way to supply vitamins, minerals and other nutrients in an easily digestible way before embarking on a full fibre diet.

Mucous colitis is another type of colitis which shows itself in the secretion of mucus and in some cases, blood, in the stools. Constipation is the first sign, with severe pains in the abdomen following afterwards. It is thought that this kind of colitis is triggered off by nervous tension and stress. Some people are more predisposed to this than others, but many of us are affected by stress at some stage in our lives and this condition could be the result. Eating a poor selection of food, including junk and convenience foods, is another cause of the illness. If it is acute, the patient should have complete rest and relaxation so that both mind and body are given a chance to recover from the nervous tension that has been felt. After finding the cause of the irritation, the diet must be worked out to give the patient a chance to recover permanently. Short-term remedies are never the full answer.

There is yet another type of colitis — which is ulcerative. This happens when the mucous membrane of the large intestine becomes inflamed and then ulcerated. There are no typical cases of symptoms for this particular condition — doctors find that it varies with each individual patient. Therefore the treatment has to be based on the individual and no generalizations can be made.

Various juices can be taken, from warm water and lemon juice, on rising, with either a 5 fl oz (140ml) glass of apple or orange juice (orange is also good, for it is slightly laxative). Breakfast can include wholemeal toast thinly spread with vegetable margarine and some muesli which can be soaked with fruit juice and topped with yogurt, a fine supplier of the B vitamins for nervous conditions. Carrot (or carrot and celery juice) can be taken in 5 fl oz (140ml) glasses during the morning and afternoon, and before going to bed. If tea is liked, it should be herb tea, sweetened with just a little honey if necessary. Lunch and dinner menus can gradually build up the fibre that is needed for full health. Other juices which are good for colitis are beetroot, pear, apricot, peach and pineapple.

5

Raw Juice Drinks

Instead of simply taking 'straight' juices, however nutritious and refreshing they may be, there will probably be even more benefit from making up healthy cocktails which are also extremely tasty.

For example, take equal parts of apple and apricot juice, or the same quantities of apple and grape, or pear and prune juice. Or try two parts apple and one part cherry juice. Or three parts tomato and one part celery juice.

Mix up equal amounts of pineapple and peach juice for a really refreshing and delicious drink. For a tangy taste, try equal quantities of apple and grapefruit juice. For a real taste of summer, enjoy equal quantities of strawberry and apricot juice. There are lots more combinations to try out. It's almost possible to imagine oneself at a health farm, when enjoying a really healthy vegetable cocktail, with three parts carrot juice to one part spinach juice.

Serve the natural cocktail in an attractive glass and garnish it with a sprig of scented mint, a slice of lemon or orange floating on top. Sprinkle some chopped parsley, mint or chives over it if preferred. Make the drink look tempting and then sip it slowly, enjoying its delicate aroma and flavour, which is helping the digestion at the same time.

Add other ingredients to make healthy drinks — the additions to the juice making it more of a snack than a drink. Use honey, egg yolks, yogurt or brewer's yeast and invent combinations for drinks. Here are a few ideas:

High-Protein Drink

Mix together one dessertspoonful of whey powder, one dessertspoonful of powdered brewer's yeast into a glass of water three-quarters full. To this add two tablespoons of acid or sub-acid fruit juice of choice. This is a drink that is ideal as a protein supplement for anyone, but especially for growing children.

Fruit Yogurt

Add two tablespoons of fruit juice, and honey to taste, to half a pint of plain yogurt. This is excellent as it is easy to digest and a good way of giving natural yogurt to children. It would be ideal as a pudding or a snack.

Body Building Tonic

This is also a very good and nutritious drink for people recovering from an illness. Beat an egg yolk into a glass of fresh chilled orange juice. Some brewer's yeast or wheatgerm and a teaspoon of honey may be added.

Slimmer's Cocktail

Into a glass of chilled grapefruit juice mix a dessertspoon of powdered brewer's yeast. This can form a part of a slimming diet and can help stave off craving for food if it is sipped between meals.

Natural Punch

A dozen oranges and between six and eight lemons are needed

for this delectable drink. When they have been put through the juicer, add four quarts of iced water and sweeten with a little honey. Serve with a slice of orange on top and this makes not only a thirst-quencher for hot days but a wonderful way of taking vitamin C on colder ones to guard against winter colds.

Almond Cup

For this drink a little almond butter is needed; this is made in the same way as brandy butter, by beating up butter and ground almonds. Add a teaspoon of the almond butter to a cup of freshly chilled juice — choose between orange, apple, pineapple or grape juice. Beat it all up until it is frothy.

Oatmeal Surprise

So called because it seems an unlikely ingredient in a drink, even a health drink, and more surprisingly it is absolutely delicious. Soak one tablespoon of rolled oats or oatmeal in a pint of water. Leave it for a few hours or overnight. Drain off the water and chill. Add the juice of a lemon and some honey to taste and stir well.

General Points on Juices

One cucumber will give quite a lot of juice in comparison with other vegetables. It is vastly improved by adding a little lemon juice and honey. Celery juice is rather strong, so it is best used with other juices. Use the leaves as well as the sticks of celery. Tomato juice combines well with yogurt. Grape juice or pineapple juice make delightful bases for fresh fruit salads. Add parsley or mint to carrot or tomato juice. Spinach juice can be added to other juices or whisked up with yogurt. Use small handfuls of leaves and stalks in the juice extractor. It is also rather strong, so it needs to be taken in combination with other juices. Watercress is very concentrated, so is best used in a mixture. Feed the washed stalks and leaves in small bunches into the juicer, adding a little water.

Some other combination juice ideas:
    Carrot and apple (five parts carrot to three parts apple)
    Carrot (eight parts), beet (two parts) and cucumber (three parts)
    Carrot (seven parts), celery (five parts) and spinach (four parts)
    Carrot (eight parts) to four parts each of cabbage and lettuce

Amounts of raw vegetables and fruits needed:
    1 lb (450g) carrots makes ⅓ pint (200ml) juice
    1 lb (450g) apples makes ⅓ pint (200ml) juice
    1 lb (450g) tomatoes makes ½ pint (300ml) juice
    1 lb (450g) blackberries makes ½ pint (300ml) juice
For normal juice drinking, that is, for health and pleasure rather than therapy, a pint of juice a day is recommended.

The next selection of recipes are very evocative of lazy summer days spent watching birds and butterflies in the garden, with the heavy scent of flowers all around. Well, one can dream occasionally!

Iced Mint
4 oz (100g) fresh mint leaves
3 oz (75g) sugar or honey
3 lemons

Juice the lemons, and pound the mint leaves with a pestle and mortar, if available, otherwise chop finely and use a rolling pin or meat tenderizer to pound them on a board.

Add an ounce (25g) of the sugar and pound it again. Make a syrup by boiling the sugar or honey in a litre (1¾ pints) of water for five minutes.

Take the pan away from the heat, allow to cool, then add the lemon juice and mint pulp. Stir well and chill for several hours before serving.

Hop Lemonade
½ oz (15g) fresh hops or ¼ oz (7g) dried hops
Small piece bruised ginger
Bunch fresh apple or other type of mint
1 thinly sliced lemon
4 oz (100g) raw sugar — honey if preferred

Fill a large pan with 2 litres (3½ pints) cold water and add all the other ingredients except the sugar. Bring to the boil and turn down to a rapid simmer for half an hour. This will reduce the liquid to half. Strain, then stir in the sugar, or honey, until it is dissolved. Boil for another five minutes, then pour off into a jug and leave to cool. Serve chilled with a sprig of mint on top.

Home-made Lemonade
4 lemons
6 oz (175ml) raw brown sugar or honey
1½ pints (900ml) boiling water

Scrub the lemons, halve them, then squeeze the juice by hand or in an electric citrus juicer. Place the juice and the pulp in a large bowl with the sugar or honey and pour ½ pint of boiling water over. Stir until the sugar or honey dissolves. Add the lemon halves and another pint of boiling water. Stir well, then cover and leave to cool. Strain, squeezing out the juice from the lemon halves and serve. This makes 1½ pints of lemonade.

This lemonade may need to be more diluted, to taste, especially for children.

Pineapple or Orange Thirst-Quencher
½ cup pineapple or orange to each person
¼ cup of the juice of either fruit for each person
Squeeze of lemon juice and some ice for each serving

Peel the fruit and remove the pips. Cut up into chunks and blend with the juice and a squeeze of lemon until it is smooth. Add the ice and mix it until the cubes are crushed. Serve it in a tall elegant glass with a sprig of mint and a slice of orange or pineapple.

Dried Fruit Shake
2 oz (55g) dried fruit, of either apricots, peaches, pears, prunes or dates
A cup or two of warm water
Squeeze of lemon
Some honey

Soak the dried fruit for several hours in the water. A mixture of fruit can be used, and it is easy to use some dried fruit compote which can be bought in a packet from a health food store. Pour the fruit and water into a blender and whisk until smooth. Add a little lemon and the honey if desired and also some added flavouring: a pinch of cinnamon or a drop of vanilla essence.

Lemon or Orange Fizz
Wash and chop half a lemon or orange and drop into the electric blender. After pouring on enough water just to cover the fruit, blend it until it is smooth. Strain through a nylon sieve into a glass or jug and top up with mineral water. This

may be sweetened with honey, according to taste.

Milk and yogurt make great additions to the home juicer's repertoire. Try adding a quarter of a pint of milk and the same amount of natural yogurt to one or two teaspoons of honey (to taste) and blending in the liquidizer. It is best served chilled.

Alternatively, pour 4 fl oz (100ml) fruit or vegetable juice into a liquidizer, with 3 fl oz (75ml) of fresh milk and the same amount of natural yogurt. Blend until smooth, adding a little honey if liked, and serve the drink chilled.

Yogurt Milk and Fruit Special
4 oz (100g) fresh fruit — strawberries, raspberries, apricots, peaches, any fruit of choice
¼ pt (140ml) natural yogurt
½ pt (285ml) milk
Raw sugar or honey to taste (optional)

Prepare the fruit, washing it well and removing any stones and stalks. Place all the ingredients into the liquidizer and blend until smooth. Chill and sieve before serving, if a smooth drink is liked; otherwise do not waste the pulpy bits — eat it with a spoon.

Juices That Do Not Combine Well
While so many fruit and vegetables complement each other and make delicious juices, there are some that do not go well together. Here is a list as a guide:

Apricot juice should not be used with juice extracted from green vegetables, such as cabbage.

Blackberry juice should not be used with juice extracted

from beetroot or the tops of beetroot.

Fig juice is incompatible with radish juice.

Grape juice should not be mixed with carrot juice.

Citrus juices, such as grapefruit, orange or lemon, do not go with cabbage, watercress or turnip top juice.

Pear and tomato juices are incompatible.

Do not take prune juice with cabbage, watercress or onion juice.

There is no great danger if any of these combinations are taken, but they will probably upset the digestion and make life temporarily uncomfortable.

Index